CONTENTS

COPPERNICKEL

number 20 / spring 2015

EDITOR/MANAGING EDITOR
Wayne Miller

EDITORS, POETRY
Brian Barker
Nicky Beer

EDITORS, FICTION
Teague Bohlen
Joanna Luloff

EDITOR, NONFICTION
Joanna Luloff

ASSOCIATE EDITORS
Steven Dawson
Courtney Harrell
Emily Jessen
Kyra Scrimgeour

ASSISTANT EDITORS
Erin Brackett
Haleigh Cannalte
Jacqueline Gallegos
Maggie Gelbwaks
Meredith Herndon
Taylor Hine
Tucker King
Jennifer Loyd
Lyn Poats
Nicholas Ramsey
Ariel Sullivan
Carley Tacker

CONTRIBUTING EDITORS
Mark Brazaitis
Geoffrey Brock
A. Papatya Bucak
Victoria Chang
Robin Ekiss
Tarfia Faizullah
V. V. Ganeshananthan
Kevin Haworth
Joy Katz
David Keplinger
Jesse Lee Kercheval
Jason Koo
Thomas Legendre
Randall Mann
Adrian Matejka
Pedro Ponce
Kevin Prufer
Frederick Reiken
James Richardson

ART CONSULTANT
Maria Elena Buszek

OFFICE MANAGERS
Elaine Beemer
Francine Olivas-Zarate

Copper Nickel is the national literary journal housed at the University of Colorado Denver. Published in March and September, it features poetry, fiction, essays, and work in translation by established and emerging writers. We welcome submissions from all writers. Submissions are assumed to be original and unpublished. For more information, please visit www.copper-nickel.org. Subscriptions are available—and at discounted rates for students—at www.regonline.com/coppernickelsubscriptions. *Copper Nickel* is distributed to subscribers and through Publishers Group West and Media Solutions. We are deeply grateful for the support of the Department of English and the College of Liberal Arts & Sciences at the University of Colorado Denver.

TRANSLATION FOLIOS

On the Cover / Cortney Andrews, *Double Fold*, C-Print, 2012

(to view more of Andrews' work, visit www.cortneyandrews.com)

Editor's Note:

THIS ISSUE MARKS THE RELAUNCH of *Copper Nickel* after a period of hiatus, which—as many of our readers know—was brought on by the tragic and sudden death of the journal's founder, Jake Adam York, in 2012.

Both Jake and his work were well known in literary circles and beyond. His was a large and generous personality, and his striking, ambitious, and often deeply moral poems only continue to grow in their importance to the conversation of American letters. At the time of this writing, *Abide*—his posthumous fourth collection—is a finalist for the National Book Critics Circle Award. If you haven't read it, I urge you to do so.

In relaunching *Copper Nickel,* my co-editors and I have tried to build on the legacy of the journal while also striking out for new ground. We continue to aspire toward diversity and eclecticism, printing work that appeals to us regardless of aesthetic affiliation, and we also continue to be particularly (though by no means exclusively) interested—as Jake was—in work that considers sociohistorical context. In these ways, *Copper Nickel* hasn't changed.

We have, however, slightly altered our look and format (as you might notice), and right out of the gate we've added a recurring feature—the "Translation Folio," in which a translator introduces and contextualizes several poems or a piece of prose by an author writing in a language other than English. Given that American literature can sometimes tend toward insularity, or even isolationism, we like to see American writing in contact with international work, which is the overarching goal of this sort of feature.

There have been other changes as well. Among them: (1) *Copper Nickel* has expanded its national distribution and should increasingly be available in bookstores across the country. (2) We've added a roster of contributing editors, whose input we're grateful for. And (3) we're in the process of enhancing our online presence, which already includes a new subscription manager (www.regonline.com/coppernickelsubscriptions—tell your friends!) and, in the not-too-distant future, will include a new website with regularly updating content.

Above all else, our primary goal moving forward is to raise the profile of *Copper Nickel* incrementally, consistently, and responsibly, both to honor Jake's long-term vision as founder and—equally important—to find an ever-larger audience for the extraordinary authors we print. We hope you'll continue to follow us as we develop further over the next few years. All of us here at *Copper Nickel* are very excited about where we're headed.

—Wayne Miller

JOEL BROUWER

The New New Normal

In one of his lives the Buddha
came upon a starving tigress about
to eat her cubs in desperation,
and cast his body down a ravine
to break it open for the creature to eat.
By July the young fox no longer flees
as I approach on my morning walk,
and is no longer young. I find her scat
on the path, black with blackberries.
Everyone I know loves these stories no matter
how many times I tell them. No one I know
seems too upset about the government
collecting our data. It is happening, it has
happened, it will happen, it will have happened,
again I nod off over my conjugations and
learn nothing. For a long time I've been
cycling in samsara, wasting countless
lives, sometimes due to excessive desire
and sometimes to ignorance. Last night
I read a book by a Vietnam POW. Alone
for weeks at a time in his cell, he built
imaginary houses, board by board,
nail by nail. Let's say there is a hell.
Do you suppose it gets gradually
less hellish, as one year melts into
the next? Or does the Devil have some trick
to keep the horror eternally fresh?
The POW took care not to skip any steps
as he worked, and to think about each task
for as long as it would take to do back
on earth. I crouch—slowly, slowly—
to the turf at the foot of a myrtle,

and the fox folds her long back legs
and sits to face me. He pounded two nails
each into five thousand shingles,
but when he finished a house, he didn't
imagine moving into it, having a party
in the backyard, kissing his kids.
He started building another one next door.
By the end of the war he had a whole
empty neighborhood in his head. The fox
is just at the edge of the woods and
could vanish in a flash. But this morning
we both want to think on this issue
a little, this question of whether anything
happens just once. After his sacrifice
the Buddha's family wept at his loss
but he wasn't lost! He had been reborn
in the celestial realm of Tushita.
What did you do during the war? I watched
a lot of documentaries and spoke almost
exclusively in the subjunctive mood.

Lines Written in Berlin

When the Wall fell Berliners feared thousands
of de-mobbed patrol dogs would go feral
in the streets, but once they'd been adopted
by idealistic families, fed
soft food, permitted to sleep on sofas,
the dogs soon took to post-historical life
and learned to fetch the sticks that children threw.
I meant to put a pebble on Brecht's grave
but found it perfect as it was, a rough
dark unpolished boulder, the name in crisp
white sans-serif. The brutal colliding
with style to distract us from the rot
beneath our feet. It takes just a little
longer than a lifetime to learn to die.
Only when out for walks where the Wall had stood
were the dogs jerked back to false consciousness.
Undistractible, intractable, they paced
their former courses with mechanical precision,
even along passages where no trace
or ruins remained. They could not be retrained.
I found a psychology textbook lying
on the sidewalk and picked it up, thinking
I might learn something, but someone had
hollowed it out, I think to hide dope in,
because you could still smell the faint
mint stain of it. So that was what I learned.

MICHELLE OAKES

Bionics

She shows the class her robot arm
each time they ask. They like the science
of her old arm's phantom—
how the doctors taught her nerves
to speak to the machine. She wants
the new wrist to turn, to face the hand
palm up, and the phantom turns it.

This arm is hers, but at the lab
they're working on a better arm—its fingers touch
as if they feel. She watches herself move
in the mirror. She knows that woman
isn't her. Still, she's no one else.
One day, she'll squeeze a paper cup
just enough to hold it.

How to Live

There was a time
when a horse-drawn circus-trailer full of monkeys
fell off a bridge. It was a rope bridge
                                    suspended over a gorge

that terminated in rapids.
A rope broke or a horse shied;
                            either way,

all of the monkeys drowned.

                        •

All over the country, circus performers were falling.

A famous equestrienne, aware of the current danger,
conceded to leave off
wearing her usual gorgeous
                        full-length satin evening gown, performing, once,

in pants.
            She was as graceful and lovely as ever, but her second horse
broke, and she failed to land

her final backwards somersault.

Newspapermen tried to record the phenomenon.

Documents exist—accounts,
personal and revealing, detailed, anecdotal—
                                but the papers always ran:

X. falls from [   ] in [   ];
hospitalized last night,
released this morning.

                        •

Here, now, a blue-jay seems to fall,
                              over and over,

out of the tree-branch above my head.
I feed it pistachios.

It carries a nut
back to its branch,
shells it and eats it.

From below, it looks an entirely different bird—
                              fat and furred—

         •

forget about birds.

Somewhere, even now, a real, human aerialist is attempting the sky.

CATHERINE PIERCE

Disaster Work

Someone is on the plane
that noses 2,000 feet into the air, stops,
then drops. Someone is in
the tornado-flattened Texaco station.
Someone is on the bus the suicidal
or stroke-struck driver launches
through the guardrail and off the mountain.

It isn't you. You're watching
a ticker scroll placidly across
the bottom of the screen, thinking
awful, awful, and below those words,
deeper than articulation can go,
hums your golden gratitude
that once again this is a tragedy

you can witness but not touch.
You can continue the work
of chewing your waffle. You can
approach the smoothed edges
of disaster, and you can,
when you light on a rough spot—
the image of the little boy's

brown shoe in the rubble, the woman
who looks like your mother
howling in a blue hat—pull back.
Some will say this is cowardice,
your unwillingness to hold
these horrors in your hands. But
if you considered, truly, the dead child,

the husband that the woman
who looks like your mother
will never see again; if you considered,
truly, what it means that a plane
could drop without warning
with its full load of daughters
and coaches and magazine-readers,

that the sky might unfold a beast
that will hunt you without reason,
that the white-mustached man
behind the wheel of your bus
is not programmed but is a human
stranger you have chosen to trust
with your absurdly flimsy life—

how in the world could you do
the work of chewing your waffle?
How could you do the impossible work
of putting your child to bed,
saying goodnight, closing the door
on the darkness?

Alleys

Because the proper *where* for an alley is *down*.
Because down them we might disappear.

Because once you read a book in which
a man with a top hat and a maimed hand

wept—not cried, not sobbed—in an alley,
and you've been in love with that man

for 23 years now and have told no one.
Because you secretly believe that being

Jack-the-Rippered is a rock star way to go.
Because your aunt said not to. Because once

you saw a movie where lovers in black and white
tangled in an alley in Siena, only the stone

walls keeping them upright, penned in the world,
but when you went to Italy at 20, you found

catcalls and bronchitis. Because if ever the 21st
century was going to open one way and end

another, it would be down an alley: enter
from the blanched Midwest, overdue

library books, the mundanity of salons,
and exit into blue, smell of jonquils, an old lady

with a strange accent scolding you *Child! Child!*
Because you believe there are still mysteries

worth risking a throat for. Because sometimes
your world is dim and smog-covered, and you

weary of it, the lamps never bright enough,
the coffee weak, and so you force yourself

into the blackest alley in town, stride through it
with your whole store of false courage, and emerge

into the same world, lit now by undark, unbrick.

ALLISON BENIS WHITE

from "Please Bury Me in This"

I am making a world I can think inside.

Cutting faces out of paper and taping them on glass like thoughts.

Am I a monster, Clarice Lispector asked in *The Hour of the Star, or is this what it means to be human?*

To have a mind, I think as I cut another face.

What makes the shape become visible, and breathe, is the angle and variation of absence.

Sugar skull, I whisper, what I have known all along.

I am you gone.

from "Please Bury Me in This"

Or a swan's neck above an hourglass smudged with coal.

Let the darkness slip quietly to the floor.

With my head bowed and from the chest down, unbuttoning each dark pearl.

I mean the death of death leaves a hole.

Tell me everything now before you go: word by word, the mouth releases the soul.

HENRY ISRAELI

Love Letter to Albert Speer

A white page
is a thing of beauty

genetically perfect
pigment-free.

Words can only
darken its splendor.

By the fourth stanza
the page is defiled.

By the fifth
it induces repulsion.

But by the sixth
one can start

to see the beauty
of the ancient

column appearing
out of nowhere

almost miraculously
down the blank canvas

the symmetry
pleasing the primal

desire of the mind
that loves the hard

vertical, muscular
and unflinching line

that loves repetition
and order

that loves masculinity
and order

that is pleased
by the calm row

of heads lowered
feet shuffling

that move in unison
into death's embrace.

NATHAN OATES

The White Chickens

WHILE JASON PLAYED SOCCER WITH Sasha in the yard, Holly took the pile of blankets, sheets, and pillows her sister-in-law had left on the picnic table and arranged them into beds in the barn, as far as possible from the chickens, though the whole place throbbed with their clucks, their shaking and fluttering, their aborted leaps toward flight against the wire cage. Two years ago, the last time they'd been up to visit, Sasha, then three, had spent a morning in the chicken pen with Uncle Robby, picking up the birds. She'd taken to trying to catch pigeons in the park back in Brooklyn, cooing at them the way her uncle had taught. And so as soon as they'd come into the barn Sasha had gone straight to the coop.

"No!" Jason had screamed. Sasha stopped, arms out for balance.

"Don't touch those things. Don't touch them," he yelled, scooping her up.

Too frightened to ask why, Sasha looked at her mother for an explanation.

"They're dirty, honey," Holly said, trying to keep her voice even. There'd been enough shouting over the past few days. In the city, on the trip, on the ferry, and then, finally, and maybe worst of all, outside the house, when they'd called Alice.

"No, they're not!" Sasha cried.

Holly had heard Robby tell the girl how chickens were actually clean animals. But times had changed, and it was too much to explain, so she just let Jason carry their girl out into the yard.

The blankets laid down, Holly went out to watch them play, but she couldn't stop looking at the house, from inside of which Alice was surely watching, probably with her new baby Anabel clutched to her chest. Maybe if they'd left the city immediately, before the riots, before the quarantines, before the shooting on the bridge, and especially before those images on the news of body bags, thousands of them, dumped into a construction site behind a hospital in Queens, if they'd gotten out before all that, maybe Alice would've let them into the house. Though Holly knew what Jason would say. No fucking way. His older brother's wife was a bitch. That's what he called her after the phone call in the driveway, and though she hated that word she didn't say anything, because she'd seen the panic edging up in his eyes. It had started there last night, as they'd driven through upstate New York, past shuttered towns, through check-points where the policemen wore surgical masks and pointed flashlights into their eyes. They'd assumed things were better outside the city, but that's not how it looked as they drove, waiting in the long lines at the gas stations the government had taken over. All the fear and stress he'd pent up for weeks had come surging out after that phone call from the driveway.

But she felt he'd earned a moment of hysterics after holding it together long enough to get them out of the city, getting them all the way up here. He was the one who'd decided they should drive out Long Island and catch one of the ferries she'd never even heard of up into Connecticut. The next day, they'd heard on the radio, those ferries had been shut down, sealing off the island. Temporarily, the news insisted, but by then everyone knew not to trust what you were told.

"Who's hungry?" Holly shouted, and Jason carried the squirming Sasha over.

The lasagna was frozen on the inside, surely because Alice had been rushing to get it out there before they arrived. Wouldn't want them to actually, you know, *see* her. Alice had asked them to call when they arrived, in case she was out doing errands. Robby wasn't home: like every other doctor in America, or maybe now the world, he was swamped.

As they'd pulled up the long gravel drive Jason had asked Holly to make the call. A weak, "Hello?" came after two rings.

"Alice," Holly said, as brightly as she could through the descending pall of exhaustion. They'd made it. The lovely wooden house with its dark green shutters and screen porch was right there in front of them.

"Are you here?" Alice said, her voice tight and hard.

"We are," Holly said. Even then, she could tell something wasn't right. "Are you?"

"What?"

"Are you home?" Holly leaned forward and through the leaded glass windows, shimmering gray with the sky, she thought she saw something move.

"I don't know. I," but Alice stopped.

"Excuse me?" Holly said.

"I left you some food, outside. And blankets. On the table. Can you see it?"

Between the house and the barn was the picnic table, atop it the lasagna, covered with tin foil, and the heap of blankets.

"What? Food?"

"Robby and I have been talking," Alice began.

She said something else, but just then Jason said, "What the hell is going on?" and reached for the phone.

Holly leaned away from his hand and said, "Wait, I'm sorry, Alice. What?"

"Just until we're sure you're not sick," Alice said.

"What are you saying?" Holly said, leaning against the window.

"The barn's winterized. We keep the goats and chickens out there all winter. And it's been warm. You'll be fine."

"The barn?"

"What? What the fuck? No fucking way," Jason shouted, throwing open his door.

"Just for a few days. Robby said the incubation period is seven days. So after that, well, we'll know."

"If we're sick," Holly said, watching her husband walk toward the house.

"You have to understand," Alice said. "Anabel's so little. Last week five babies died at the hospital. And there aren't even any quarantines up here."

"You want us to live in the barn for a week?" Holly said. Jason climbed the steps and pounded on the door with his fist. Holly could hear the banging through the phone.

"Robby will be home tonight. He'll talk to you about it," Alice said over Jason's shouting, coming to Holly in stereo.

She looked into the back seat. Sasha stared at her portable DVD player, headphones covering most of her head.

Jason pointed at the door, mimed something. Holly shook her head.

"Robby will be home," Alice said, then hung up.

"What the fuck is going on?" Jason shouted, pounding down the steps. "Seriously? What the fuck?"

When Holly tried to explain he immediately started shaking his head and shouting, "The barn? What are we, her fucking goats?"

He said he was going to smash in the window, get in that way, but she knew he'd calm down quickly, for Sasha, and he did, lifted her out of the car, explaining that they couldn't go inside yet, but the barn was open, let's go see.

After dinner they went inside to look at the sleeping arrangements.

"Not so different from the Tribeca Grand," he said, holding the soccer ball under his arm. "And like the Grand they'll probably charge us seven dollars for a bottle of water."

In his sagging white T-shirt he looked thin, wasted. She knew she looked no better, in the blue and white striped shirt she'd been wearing for three days. They might look sick, but they weren't. At least as far as they knew. They were just skinny because for the past two weeks there'd barely been time to think about eating, barely time to think about anything other than the fear of contagion.

Sasha jumped into the pile of blankets and rolled around, twisting them together, undoing all the work, but Holly couldn't bring herself to complain. Cooler air blew in through the doors, and Jason hauled them shut, then turned on the heaters.

Holly cuddled with Sasha in the pile of blankets, reading her the books they'd grabbed before leaving the apartment. *Harold and the Purple Crayon*, *Curious George and the Firefighters*, *Dodsworth in London*. None were favorites, but Sasha didn't complain. Holly sang "Rocky Raccoon" until she could slip out and join Jason at the window. Cool air leaked in through the glass. It was April, almost spring even that far north, but it could still snow. It happened up here, all the way through May, a sudden Arctic blast.

"Brotherly love, right?" Jason said, pulling Holly against him. He smelled like grease, body odor, and the coppery tang of fear.

"At least we're here," she said, kissing his neck. "At least we're safe."

"Right," he said, sarcastically, but it was true, they were safe. Unless, during the night, or tomorrow, or any time in the coming week, one of them got a sudden, spiking fever. She'd seen it happen on the subway. The young woman sitting across from her on the F hadn't looked well when she'd gotten on at 14th Street and by the time they were rattling under the river sweat stood out on her forehead, dampening her temples and her cheeks flared a bright red. The woman lurched up as the train pulled into Jay-Metrotech and fell into the man in front of her and slipped to the floor. Holly got off the train, hurried up the stairs, away from the shouting. She ran up the last flight to the street and down the block, looking back, as if that woman would come after her, cough on her face.

From outside came the snuffling of the goats. Alice's Facebook page was little more than a weekly updating on the new wonders of Anabel and the goats.

"We should sleep," she said.

"I have to talk to Rob. This," he nodded over at Sasha. "This is just bullshit."

"They're just scared."

"And assholes. Don't forget that part."

"That's true. They are kind of assholes."

"But then some things never change," Jason said. "Alice always was a bitch."

She felt suddenly dizzy, as if she might fall down, and terror rose up in her. But she touched her forehead and found it cool. She was just tired. She'd slept a couple hours on the drive, but otherwise not at all for two days.

Behind them one of the chickens started warbling, thrusting out its chest. She'd always thought of chickens as little, but these were huge. They had heavy bodies, long, proud necks, and gleaming white feathers. Robby raised them for their meat, she remembered, though the slaughtering was done elsewhere.

"I should fucking kill those things," Jason said.

"I can't believe they still have them," she said. Sleep. She needed to sleep.

"Seriously. I'm going to." He wrung his hands together, baring his teeth.

"Aren't they heritage chickens?"

"I don't care. I don't give a shit what they are," Jason said.

Holly went as steadily as she could to the blankets. She checked her forehead again before plunging down into sleep.

•

Jason was at the window when she woke up, his face almost pressed to the glass. "He's back," he said.

Her back was stiff and her head throbbed, but she forced herself up. Dawn was coming and everything was drenched with a thick, quivering blue. Tendrils of fog slipped between the trees beyond the house.

Robby came out onto the porch and looked at them through the window. He lifted his hand, then dropped it quickly, as if realizing they weren't people he knew.

Jason stepped out, then stuck his head back in and whispered, "Off for an audience with the king." Robby came down the porch steps but didn't cross the yard. There was no hug, no real greeting, just the brothers facing each other across the white fence. They didn't even seem to be talking, but then Jason faced away from her, and when Robby shook his head, rubbed his eyes, held out his hands and started to talk, she knew her husband must've been stating their case. Their case for not being treated like animals. To be treated like family.

She went to the just-open door and leaned her head against it to hear what they were saying, but it was all whispers and the sounds only came in snips. Robby turned and went into the house and Jason came back to the barn.

"What happened?" she said.

He took a deep breath, held it, then rubbed his flat palms along his temples. "Do you think he knows what an asshole he is?" Jason stared at Sasha, asleep in the blankets. "He's so calm and logical. I want to choke his fucking neck."

"Did you ask him about the chickens?"

"Of course I did. I said, 'Any chance you can get your filthy vermin out of the barn, just, you know, while we're sleeping there.' He said he'd ask Alice. Wouldn't want to make a move without the queen's permission."

They looked at the chickens. Most seemed to be dozing, a few shuffled listlessly through the sawdust. As far as anyone knew, the virus had jumped from chickens to humans at a processing plant in the Wuhan province. She remembered hearing reports on the news: thirty-six dead of bird flu in central China. Then, a sudden surge: one hundred and twelve confirmed dead, and the virus now found in Taiwan, and Hong Kong. Four hundred and fifty dead, and the United States and Europe imposed a ban on flights from China. Independent Television produced a story about the devastation in North Korea, into which the virus had slipped, with reports of mass graves, and the systematic extermination of the sick. By then the virus had already gotten into New York, though no one knew it then.

Jason kissed her head and said, "He said the real risk is to babies. And old people. That if it wasn't for Anabel he'd let us in. I asked why he got to go inside, since he's at the hospital all day. He said he wears a suit. Like a hazmat suit. And he takes a scalding shower with disinfectant. He showed me his hands, how they were all cracked and raw.

And he says he doesn't go near Anabel. He sleeps in the basement. So at least we're not the only ones cast out by the queen."

"You have to sleep, honey," she said. The tide of exhaustion was pushing up over her again and she put her head on his shoulder.

"Who's going to guard my girls," he said, "if I do that?"

"We're safe now, honey. We're safe," she said, tugging him over toward the blankets.

•

By the time Sasha woke up breakfast was on the picnic table: pancakes, wrapped in tinfoil so they were still warm, a stick of butter, and a bottle of maple syrup. Holly felt like crying when she took the first bite. Sure, they were in the barn, and that wasn't ideal, but they were out of New York. She'd never wanted to live anywhere else in her adult life, but once the flu started spreading—she saw it as a red stain, seeping up the avenues, leaping over entire blocks—the city had turned against them.

They used the barn's bathroom and shower, Sasha squealing about the hot water, then walked away from the house, down into the fields. It was warmer than it'd been in weeks. Some people said the flu might fade in the summer, while others worried it might mutate and cause fresh outbreaks.

Despite her terror of ticks, Holly let Sasha run through the high grass, Jason chasing after, roaring like a bear. They could hear the river long before they could see it and Sasha kept ducking into the bushes to look for it, emerging back on the trail with snips of branches and burrs—and, surely, ticks—in her dark, curly hair. Then the trail turned and they were beside the water. On an open patch of grass, they ate the sandwiches Jason had made with supplies left out beside the pancakes.

Sasha raced up and down the bank looking for fish, shouting, "Mommy, I see it, I see a fish, Mommy, I see it!" and hopping with her hands near her mouth in astonishment. Every time she'd seen those stupid subway ads for a storage company—"Raising a child in a New York apartment is like raising an oak tree in a thimble."—she'd thought, *Oh, fuck off.* She'd been raised in the suburbs and had hated it. But now, seeing Sasha running free, it was clear that this *was* the natural world of the child, the world of the woods, all that creepy mystery. Jason had grown up like this in Wisconsin, and the way he played with Sasha, ducking under the branches of the trees, made her wonder if he wished they'd chosen this life.

She lay back, watched the sky through the branches, feeling calm for the first time in months, and she must've fallen asleep, because when she opened her eyes Jason was standing above her with Sasha clinging to his neck.

"We have to go," he said, in that tone she'd grown used to.

"What?" she said, sitting up, a lurch of nausea in her throat.

"Just pack up," he said, then started back down the path. Holly watched them until she could see Sasha's face. Her cheeks were bright red.

Holly flailed around, grabbing the things they'd scattered in their picnic. Jason was almost to the barn before she caught up.

"What is it?" Holly said, gasping.

"She's hot," he said, breaking into a run.

"Hot?" she shouted, but he didn't answer.

In the dark of the barn he laid Sasha atop the blankets. She curled into a ball, a blob of drool on her cheek where it had pressed to her dad's shoulder. Her breathing was fast. Sweat slicked her hair to her temples.

"What's wrong with her?" Holly said. She wanted to pick Sasha up, squeeze out whatever was wrong, but knew she shouldn't get too close, that would just make her hotter. She needed space. Or was Holly just protecting herself? Keeping her distance. Like a monster.

"We were playing, and then she sat down and said she was dizzy. She's burning up."

"Maybe it's heat stroke. Couldn't it be the heat?"

"I don't know, Holly, I don't know." He rose and hurried out of the barn and up to the house. She could hear him pounding on the door, then shouting.

Sasha's cheeks were still flushed, but her breathing seemed to have slowed, and when Holly touched her forehead it was hot, yes, it was hot, she couldn't pretend it wasn't hot. But not burning. Not like they warned on the news, on the radio, on the internet, on the pamphlets they'd pushed under the doors of their co-op building.

"Please, honey," Holly whispered, moving closer. "Please, please, please." She took the girl's hand, her little fingers. She was still a baby. Holly's baby. She remembered the statistics. 0-5 years old: 60% survival rate. And then her own bracket: 25-45 years old: 90%. It seemed so stupid, so cruel. But it wasn't cruel. That's what Jason had insisted all through the early outbreaks. Everyone who said this was unfair, terrible, mean, those people were thinking like children, or like someone a thousand years ago, as if nature was full of malice, as if it was anything more than microbes reproducing. But it wasn't true. Jason was wrong. Not literally. Literally he was right. But it *was* cruel, now that it was their baby.

He came back from the house and knelt beside her.

"Alice is calling Robby. She said he'll bring back Tamaflu. The new version. Robby said they've had a lot better luck with it." He spoke evenly, as if it had already been settled.

"But maybe she's not sick," Holly said. "Maybe it was just the running around."

Jason squinted at Sasha. "He'll be here soon. And Alice is going to put some ice, some juice and stuff on the porch."

"So we're just supposed to wait?" She heard the panic in her own voice, shrill and wild against his calm, but she didn't care. This was their baby.

"What do you want to do?" he said, touching Sasha's arm gently.

"Go to the hospital. Right now. If she's sick, Jason, if she's sick, if she's—" but she already knew what he'd say: the hospitals were overcrowded, full of the virus.

"Calm down, sweetie. She looks better, right?" Jason said.

But Holly couldn't tell no matter how hard she stared. Sasha's breathing was quick, or maybe that was the normal rate, and her cheeks were flushed, but not that burning red she'd seen on the news, on the streets, in the faces in the cars they passed leaving New York. Without a doctor, there was no way to know. No way to know if their daughter was dying, or just tired out from the heat, from being cooped up for days, from what must've been for her a traumatic level of stress.

The sound of the car in the driveway came sooner than she expected. Jason pulled open the sliding door and Robby shouted, "Let me shower," and ran into the house.

They paced around the barn, bending over Sasha to see how she looked—still sleeping, though, now that Holly looked closely, her breathing seemed to have slowed and the redness of her cheeks was fading—and then they went to stand at the door as Robby ran across the yard. He'd put back on his scrubs and was carrying a bag with instruments, medicines maybe. He looked exhausted, and stressed, and old, his hair thickened with gray strands at the temple, and receding from his forehead.

Robby lifted Sasha's eyelids, shone a light on them. When he took his finger away the girl's eyes stayed open.

"Honey, it's OK, Uncle Robby's here," Jason said.

Robby's fingers were at her neck, taking her pulse, and Holly saw his shoulders relax. He sat back on his feet and even before he spoke, she knew what he'd say.

"She's fine," Robby said. "I can run some more tests, if you want, but this is definitely not the flu. She's just tired out."

Sasha stared at him, as if she'd been dreaming about her uncle, and now here he was.

"Let her rest. Take it easy tomorrow." Robby ran a hand over Sasha's head, and now that the threat had passed, now that his role as a doctor was over, his role as uncle returned. He was once again the uncle who'd sequestered them in the barn, or at least let them be sequestered there by his wife, an uncle who should've take them in, like family, but had treated them instead like animals. Holly knew she should be grateful. Her baby wasn't sick. Couldn't she be grateful for just a few minutes? But instead, when Robby turned to smile, expecting a nod, a returned smile of relief, she felt her tongue thicken with hate.

"Jason," she said.

He looked at her, smiling, like his brother. She pointed at the chickens, not caring if Robby saw her do it.

"Oh, yeah. Can we talk outside, Robby?" he said.

Robby looked at Holly. The message was clear: he'd left the hospital, all those truly sick people, to come back and check on their girl, who they should've been able to tell was just tired out and overheated, but they'd panicked, and now she was moving on to her next demand?

Sasha wanted to go play, but Holly said, "No, honey, you need to rest. Uncle Robby said so." That's what *she* wanted to do. To sleep. To wake up to a new, safe world. Or even the old world. Any world but this one.

Jason didn't come back immediately, and when she went to the window they were sitting at the picnic table with beers. Jason picked at his bottle's label, smiling as he talked, as if he was telling a joke.

She turned around to find Sasha at the chicken coop, her fingers through the wire, her face pressed against it.

"Honey!" Holly screamed.

A chicken dropped with a flutter from its perch and moved across the sawdust, flapping its wings sharply. Sasha wiggled her fingers through the mesh.

Holly ran over and dragged the yelping girl away from the birds, all of them up now, filling the barn with their warbling cries.

Jason came back in a few minutes later with two beers. "Thank god she's OK," he said.

"Did you ask him about the chickens?" she said, wishing she could refuse the beer until he solved this, but she already had it in her hand.

"He said they're fine. He tested them right before we got here. They're heritage birds, you know." He said this last bit in the arch, mocking tone he used to imitate his brother. But she knew his heart wasn't in it. He wasn't on her side anymore. This was how it'd always been with his brother: when their parents died two years ago, within six months of one another, Robby dominated and condescended to Jason throughout the entire process. Their parents had made Robby the executor of the will and he'd only relinquished what he didn't need, like the battered old Corolla, without which, of course, they'd be stuck back in New York. But she'd always hated seeing Jason quiver before his brother, all those childhood anxieties turning him into someone she barely knew.

"They can't stay in here, Jason," she said. "Sasha was over there. At the coop."

"Look, honey. We'll deal with it. But not right now. We're all tired."

They let Sasha watch a movie on her DVD player, while they tried to read, and though she said she wasn't tired, Sasha fell asleep after in Jason's arms. Like all kids, she slept with a furious intensity, as if pushing her way down through the layers of dream, pursuing something that Holly, with her numb, adult mind, had forgotten was even to be desired.

•

BY LUNCH THE NEXT DAY Sasha was bored and caught in a loop of whining—she wanted to go the river, why couldn't she go to the river?—and Jason snapped several times. They slept restlessly that night, the chickens shuffling and squawking, and the following morning Jason said, "We've got to get out of here. Just for a little while. Let's take a drive."

"Where?" Holly said.

Sasha was spooning up cereal, listening intently.

"We'll just get out of this yard for a little while, right Sasha?"

"Yes, yes, yes! Can we, Mommy?"

Holly hated how he did that, turned the girl against her, and anyway, should they really be wasting gas, but she let it go and helped them pack up the car, got Sasha dressed, and soon they were heading down the gravel drive and onto the dirt road. In only a few seconds they were out of sight of the house, and Jason was right, it felt good to rush under the bright green leaves through the scatter of shadows, then out onto the asphalt road, past the little restaurant they'd eaten at years ago, which looked closed, but of course it was, it was still morning. Not far past the town Jason turned onto a dirt road that took them over a wooden covered bridge. They went on into the next town. All the shops were closed up, no one on the sidewalks except an old man who leaned against a parking meter, head sagging.

"Too bad we can't stop somewhere," Jason said. "Get some i-c-e c-r-e-a-m."

"What?" Sasha shouted from the back.

"Nothing, honey," Holly said, frowning at Jason.

"I'm just saying it'd be nice. Creamy, melting in the mouth," he said.

"Ice cream? Are you talking about ice cream?" Sasha said.

"No, honey, Daddy's teasing," Holly said.

Sasha pouted, crossing her arms dramatically across her chest.

"Maple cremees," Jason crooned.

"It's not open, honey," Holly said to Sasha. "It's only open in the summer." She didn't say anything about the fact that attached to the cremee stand was a farm-zoo with filthy chickens and mangy goats. The girl probably remembered them fondly, despite the peck she'd gotten from a mother chicken when she'd chased a flock of chicks.

Jason turned onto a dirt road and smiled. "We'll just stop by. If it's open, well, you know, we might just have to."

"Yay!" Sasha shouted from the back, clapping.

Holly could see the parking lot was empty from down the road, and that the place was closed was soon obvious. A sheet of plastic flapped loose from one window, a piece of plywood nailed over another, and yellow police tape across the front doors, a sagging x. Where once there had been animals—goats, chickens, a donkey with a sign on his gate, "I BITE!"—were now empty coops and overgrown fields with fallen fences. But Jason pulled into the lot anyway.

"Daddy, let me out." Sasha writhed in her booster seat, plucking at the straps.

"It's closed, honey," Holly said. She turned to Jason and said, "Go. Right now."

"But I wanted a cremee!" Sasha screamed.

Hands on the wheel, Jason stared at the building. The windows were smoked over with grime and dust, but Holly thought she saw something, a shape moving inside.

"Let's go Jason, now," Holly said, watching the door, waiting to see the handle turn, to see the old woman who ran the place stumble out, bleeding from her mouth, as the sick did in their last days, stains spread over her shirt as she reached for them.

Sasha thrashed in her car seat as they pulled out, wailing, but by the time they reached the farm she'd quieted down, and when Jason lifted her from the booster seat she sagged against his shoulder. He set her down on the blankets, gave her a book to look through, and whispered to Holly, "Can you watch her? I'm going for a walk." Without waiting for an answer, he went out.

It took her a few minutes to realize what was different in the barn: the chickens were silent. She looked over at them and none were pressed up against the mesh, staring. Then she saw them, huddled in the corner, heads down.

Even as she went closer they didn't move, except to quiver. She'd seen the images on the television of the poultry processing plants in Hong Kong and South Korea. Everyone knew what a sick bird looked like now.

She grabbed Sasha, and carried her into the yard. At the head of the trail they'd hiked down two days ago Holly screamed for Jason, over and over. Sasha squirmed until she had to put the girl down.

"What are you doing, Mommy?" Sasha said, plopping down in the grass.

"Honey, stop. Just stop, OK? Just," then Holly turned and screamed for Jason.

He came running up through the trees and across the field. "What?" he gasped, clutching his knees.

"The chickens," Holly said.

"What?"

"The chickens. I think they're sick. They're just sitting there."

He looked at her, chest heaving, face red, then looked at the house.

"Wait here," he said.

The garage door was down, so he went around the side. Holly heard glass breaking, then Jason inside, tossing things aside. He came out with garbage bags in one fist, an axe in the other. On his hands he wore plastic gloves and on his face a surgical mask.

He stopped at the barn door. "Wait here."

"What's Daddy doing?" Sasha said, tugging at Holly's hand.

"It's fine, honey. He's fine. Daddy's just cleaning up."

They couldn't just stand there and listen to him kill the birds, so she put Sasha in the car and handed over the iPad. To cover the bleeping of the games she turned on the radio. The last time she'd listened had been the day they'd arrived.

MSNBC were interviewing an epidemiologist from the CDC. The scientist was describing the difficulty they were having coming up with a vaccine. The virus had already mutated several times in unexpected ways. It was quite vigorous, and adaptive, the woman said, with obvious admiration.

A summary of the news followed: the quarantine in New York had been extended to Boston, Philadelphia, and Washington D.C. Travel on the highways was restricted to emergency personnel. All flights, domestic and international, were temporarily suspended. Everyone was to stay at home. Avoid large gatherings of people. Stay away from livestock, especially pigs and birds. Temporary treatment centers had been established in most cities. If you get sick, call 911 for the closest facility.

Holly turned the dial, breathing fast. She scrolled past loud thumping pop songs. She stopped on a talk station, drawn to the urgency in the man's voice.

"They're lying, people. You get it? Lying to all of us. There's no cure and I'll tell you what, if they do come up with one, you're not going to get it. You know where it's going? To the President, Congress, those rich people who got helicoptered out of Manhattan. We should've shot them down, people. We should've gotten up on our rooftops and shot those helicopters down. Because wherever they are now, that's where the cure is going. The rest of us, we don't rate. Do you get it? In this system, in this world, we don't count. We're the people who die. They're clearing us out. And if I was you, if I was any of you out there, I'd get myself a gun, I'd hole up in my house, and if the government comes with their men in their white suits and their masks I'd put a bullet in their chests. That's what I'd do. That's what I'm going to do. I have friends in New York and you know what they tell me? Bodies in the street, people. There are bodies in the street. Just piled up there. They're giving up on us. No one, and I mean no one, is coming to save you."

Holly reached for the dial with a shaking hand, clicked the dial off, and only then noticed that Sasha was staring at the radio.

"Who was that, Mommy?" the girl said.

"No one, honey. A crazy man." Her voice was shaking. Where was Jason? What was taking so long?

"Who is he going to kill?"

"What are you talking about?" Holly said, trying not to shriek.

"He said he was going to get a gun—"

"No, honey. He was being silly. Guns are bad, honey. He was just being a silly man."

Sasha squinted at the radio, as if she could still faintly hear the lunatic's ranting.

"Play your game, sweetie," Holly said.

As if she'd summoned him with her panic, Jason stepped from the barn. He no longer wore the mask, or the gloves.

"Wait here, baby," Holly said, and got out of the car.

"They're gone," he said, looking back at the barn. He was sweating, a dark stain down the front of his gray T-shirt.

"Were they sick?"

"I don't know. I took them out back. I broke their necks. I didn't want blood everywhere. So I just," he wrung his hands together. "And it's done."

"So what do we do?"

"Nothing," he said. "We do nothing. Get Sasha. I'm going to shower."

Walking back into the barn he peeled off his shirt, the muscles in his back shifting, his ribs sticking out. All the softness and roundness of their Brooklyn life had gone out of him and he looked, from behind, like a new man.

•

NEITHER OF THEM HAD TO say what they were waiting for, and they both got up at the sound of Robby's car. Obviously Alice had called and told him what they'd done.

They watched as Robby, still in his scrubs, hurried around the corner of the garage, then stormed quickly up to the front door, glaring at the barn.

When Robby came back out, dressed now in jeans and white T-shirt, Jason was waiting for him at the white fence. Robby gestured at the barn, at the garage. She couldn't hear what they were saying, only the occasional rising tone in their words, until they started shouting.

"This is my house, Jason. This is my home. My family's in there."

"Fuck you, Robby. You put us in the barn. I'm your brother. And that's my family. Right there."

Robby rubbed his face with both hands and said something, pleading. Jason shook his head, gestured back at the barn. Robby's frown deepened, he stepped toward Jason and she could see the tension in her husband's neck, the way he set his feet farther apart.

"Are you fucking kidding?" Robby shouted. "You killed them?"

Jason said something, calm, but his hands at his sides were fists.

Robby moved toward the barn, but Jason's arm came up, hitting him in the chest. Jason shook his head. Robby looked down at the arm, then up at Jason, then he turned toward the house and said, "Out, OK? Tonight."

Holly trembled as Jason came into the barn. But not with fear. With excitement.

"He wants us out, to leave, tonight," he said.

"Where are we going to go?" Holly said, unable to whisper.

Sasha was listening, but there was no helping it. They couldn't protect her from everything forever.

"We're not going anywhere," Jason said, squatting beside the big duffel bag.

"But he said—"

"We're not leaving," Jason said. He tucked something into his pocket and stood up. She could see the shape, a long cylinder, and knew what it was: the can of mace he'd bought on the street after the police had shot people trying to cross the George Washington Bridge.

"Jason," she said. Wasn't she supposed to tell him to calm down, not to do this? But what else was there to do? Leave? Because they'd killed a few chickens?

For dinner they ate crackers and energy bars, gave the last of the milk to Sasha, and drank water from the tap.

The red sun fell against the dark line of trees before Robby emerged again. He came down the steps slowly. Contrite, she could see. Or at least not as angry as before.

"Here we go," Jason said. "Stay in here."

Holly wanted to say maybe they should just talk to him. He wouldn't kick him out, right? She left the door cracked and pressed her ear close.

"Listen," Robby said, as they met near the picnic table, where Jason had drawn him. "I don't think this is going to work."

"What's that?" Jason said.

With his back to her, she could see he'd moved the mace from his pocket and tucked it into his belt against his spine.

"This," Robby said, gesturing at the barn. "It's just." He stopped, rubbed his eyes, folded his arms across his chest. "It's not working out."

"You mean us staying in the barn?" Jason said.

Robby nodded, frowning. At Jason's expression, she was sure, though she couldn't see it. "It's not working out," Robby said. "I hoped it would, but now Alice is scared. I mean, breaking into the garage. And the chickens." His voice tightened, but he paused and kept going. "I want to help. We do. But we can't do it like this."

"Can't do what?" Jason's voice was loud, almost jocular.

"Can't let you stay here. We're going to need to have you move out of the barn."

"And go where? Where are we supposed to go, Robby? You have that planned out too?" As he spoke, Jason moved closer and Robby stumbled back over a clump of grass.

"There's a camp," Robby said. "It's nicer than this. I mean, they have trailers, mostly tents, but I think I can get you a trailer."

"A camp," Jason said, then he threw back his head and laughed, loud.

"Jason, please. My wife is in there. My baby is two months old."

"And my baby," Jason shouted, stepping closer so again Robby stumbled back, "is in there. In the barn. Where you put her. Like some kind of fucking animal. Got it, Robby? I'm looking out for my little girl. And we're not taking her to any fucking camp."

Holly could see the fear in Robby's face. His eyes darted over Jason's face, then leapt to the house, to the window, her face. She didn't move.

"Jason, listen," Robby said, stepping away again. "This is my house. You need to leave, OK? This isn't working out."

"Oh," Jason shouted, "I agree. This is definitely not fucking working out."

She watched him reach around behind and grab the mace and spray it into Robby's eyes. Robby just stood there, waiting for it to happen. Then he fell, screaming, and rolled behind the picnic table. Jason knelt over him. His fist came up, swung down.

"Come on, honey," Holly said, running to where Sasha was coloring on the floor. "Get up, honey."

"Where are we going?" Sasha said.

"We're going to the house, baby. Come on."

Sasha brushed at the straw that clung to her legs as Holly prompted her from behind so the girl wouldn't see the axe her mother had picked up and held behind her back. Robby had stopped screaming. Holly pulled open the door and saw her husband standing over his brother, who was mostly hidden by the table. She wasn't sure if Sasha had seen him. Dark was falling quickly. Holly tightened her grip on the axe.

"This way," Jason said, running over to pick up Sasha.

"I have the axe," Holly whispered, and Jason nodded.

Each carrying their load, they moved up the stone path toward the house.

MATTHEW FERRENCE

Milk Off

AT FIRST, THE REGION'S GOAT farmers were amused by our squat, knee-high Pygmies, these tightly-paunched does so different from the high-hipped loose-skinned Saanens, the cropped-ear LaManchas, the dim-faced Nubians and Alpines. With no category of their own, the Pygmies were forced to compete at the county fair directly against the larger dairy animals and presented no obstacle to their lanky struts.

My mother had taught us how to prepare, this woman who went from prim Catholic boarding school to formal Catholic women's college, whose high school rebellion amounted to the secret removal of required white gloves when visiting town. When she started a 4-H chapter that met each month in our family room, her first act was to teach farmers' children Robert's Rules of Order. She inked the words "I move" on a large rectangle of white posterboard and had my sister add a cartoon buck caught in the moment of attack, head down, curled horns pressing against the edge of the I. His instinctual act of fury signaled grammatical restraint to the club, was intended to stop us from using "motion" as a verb and, instead, contain sloppiness of voice. We were to move that the minutes of the previous meeting be accepted, to move that we lead our goats along the town's main street at the University homecoming parade. Our motion was toward refinement and clarity, learning to carry ourselves neatly in manner and language.

We learned to groom the goats as well. My mother showed us how to trim stray hairs from their udders, how to gently pull the bright links of plastic chain collars to force goat heads up, straightening their spines, how to reach an arm under goat ribs, lift, settle the animal's legs into a perfect rectangle. My sister practiced this art on her does, proven mothers to annual birthings of triplets and quads, palm-sized kids who spent part of each late winter in our mud porch, sleeping in a towel-filled cardboard box between hand feedings. My own attention turned to a young wether, his castration preventing a future of adult buckhood and guaranteeing a tender disposition. I learned how to lead him in a circle, though he rarely offered more than a sideways glance in resistance, rebellion having been cut away too.

AT THE FAIR, MY SISTER led the Pygmies again and again into the ring, where they trailed the circles of dairy goats like tiny periods at the ends of ungainly, awkwardly ostentatious sentences declaring Grand Champions and Best in Breed. Then, the most prestigious competition began, to determine the year's Best Udder.

The animals moved into the ring, sprightly sashays, high heads, tails pointed in the air. Beneath the hindquarters of each goat, the pendulous objects of examination bounced with each step. This held my eleven-year-old attention, the equally whole-some and furtive sight of girls and women dressed from head to toe in dairy whites, leading goats to be handled and judged with a limited and single-minded focus, a sorting not unlike that which would occur to me as the central concern of my junior high life in only a few years. Later, the resonance between goat and human would eventually dawn on me in a startling recognition of a different sort of goatiness, one far less wholesome, far more furtive, and far more troubling than a dozen does parading in a circle of sawdust under the gaze of a frowning, weathered judge. How odd a prim farm childhood, where the enterprise depends wholly on the production of sex, contained always to the barn, pert does tormenting our always-isolated buck, who bleated and licked the air, waiting for those rare moments when he could enjoy his release. Mostly, we avoided him, and focused our eyes on the swelling bellies of the does and appreciated the docility of my wether.

The judge watched the animals walk the circle, her eye trained to measure the standards of the American Dairy Goat Association, which favor "an attractive frame-work with femininity, strength, upstandingness, length, and smoothness of blending." The doe should be "strong yet refined" with "clean bone structure, showing freedom from coarseness." Her skin should be "thin, loose, and pliable with soft, lustrous hair." Judges are encouraged to watch for a "pleasing carriage and smoothness of walk." Later, the guidelines for my wether would focus on different attributes, points earned for animals that are "tractable" and "responsive" and "trusting" and "cooperative." The goats moved, the dairy whites, the pleasing carriages coming to a halt as the judge pointed. She bent and fingered the teats, palpated the pink flesh of udders. She selected the preliminary order, the dairy goats at the head of the judging, the Pygmy still tailing behind. A glance beneath the line revealed the justness of this decision, the heavy udders of the leaders showing off impressive, if crude, mastery. The Pygmy had no chance.

Then, someone displeased with the sorting called for a Milk Off.

The barn sprung to action, my mother alongside the others hustling into the ring carrying buckets. While my sister steadied her goat, my mother kneeled, first shaking the udder to stimulate lactation, then grabbing each teat, a pinch and a pull, until the sound of milk striking galvanized metal. The buckets frothed, and the unmistakable odor of warm sweetness mixed with sawdust and dung.

The dairy goat herders had a trick, long practiced, denying their does the relief of morning milking. Instead, they allowed the animals to engorge, heavy production dis-tending their udders. Now, those udders flopped, wrinkled teats hanging low beneath lopsided bags. The judge regarded this new information and turned to the Pygmy, whose natural state is that of the perky, the small and firm and efficient and modest udder of an animal worth noticing but who refuses to bring notice to herself.

My mother left the ring, her white 4-H t-shirt tucked neatly into clean blue jeans, her small frame moving smoothly through the gate. I do not know whether it was she who called for the milk off, or if a disgruntled dairy goat farmer hoped for a favorable reordering. Either way, the judge directed my sister and her Pygmy to the head of the line, their new and final position, declared Best Udder, while the shamed dairy goat herders considered this affront.

By THE TIME I BECAME president of the 4-H club, infatuated with the scrubbed beauty of my vice-president, the trophy won by my sister's Pygmy had long since taken permanent residence on the family room mantle. For years, I wondered why this replica milk can emblazoned with the words, Best Udder, also included the narrow etching of a stylized chicken. Eventually, my mother explained this to me, also, that the sketch signaled the form of a goat's backside, tail in the air, udder hanging beneath. She referred to this as embarrassing, as pornographic, yet for years the can remained. At meetings, she leaned the posterboard "I move" sign against the trophy, the butting buck so close to the object of his desire, but forever stalled, never quite in motion enough to reach what he longed for. My mother dusted the can carefully, arranging it just so, angling it in the sunlight to greet each visitor to our home.

MELISSA KWASNY

The Wind People

Wind people, like the buffalo,
are indigenous to our plains and demand the same fate,

the same reprisals. Burial after burial,
incremental, so that often we are too late to attend them.

But the sound of grief breaks.
The whimpering begins. The build-up, the acceleration.

Every known culture has taken upon itself
naming of the soul, usually in words for smoke or wind.

It slows us down the road in its direction.
Tourists return from the famous battlefield, chastened.

Where do the ghosts go, are they shouldering these gusts,
or, slipping our senses, do they bunker

floor-length, stooped over us but lost from our thoughts?
Who is it that manages the heavy lifting.

To lament, honor, feel shame. The composer
asks if there is a word that includes both apology and praise.

Confession perhaps, a plea for absolution. An open screen.
The shape of our violence somehow heard by us.

The Red-Winged Blackbird People

I can live with heresiarchs. I like the *here* in them and the *arch,*
the about-face, a bright badge
tossed back and forth across the fields of the party's faithful.

It is not all tragedy. It is also beauty and recovery.
Such color on the foothills. Such Italian expressions for ground—
verdaccio, imprimatura.

Rain is the preferred condition, life in the rushes.
Which we cannot penetrate without consent of its invisible rulers.
The blackbird song a pink, often heard in metaphor.

To be transparent is to be seen, to have blackbirds pass through.
Not a glass that stoppers, not glassine,
which resists, but as the eyes can make their way through light.

They are a score for brief soloists. Matches lit and blown out.
Of a piece that snags and tears and gets rewoven.
One cannot speak of blackbird and not mean thirteen—the male

colony piping, the females quieter, among leaves, brown cattail
casings over-wintered.
Thunder this morning. Geese raise their necks from the blue

bunch wheat grass they sleep in. Sky world. Our beloved terrestrial.
In between, a middle realm.
Where the blackbirds will lay their eggs in an outstretched hand.

LAURA EVE ENGEL

Memorial Day

In front of me the apple tree
is ordered. It has leaves
on its leaf parts. I say it sits
and it sits, fulfilling its
treeness as surely as it never
reads the news. I'd like
to read it the news.
Good morning, apple tree,
the morning your air's in
is in memorial. Hello, morning,
your young men are on fire
with bad ideas. Your guns
are growing into their gun
parts. And now more thoughts
arrive, disguised as this yellow
butterfly taking the act of flying
for granted as surely as I
have been unfair to young men
and that it will continue.
Today we celebrate
the apportioned dead, some
of whom were poured
on their alive mornings
into the bodies of young men.
The leaves strain in their
leaf parts, here, and in the town
I drove past to get to the tree
I'm at, town with *those dead
children* poured inside
its name. I say it and it
can be any one of. Inside
and outside of a young man

and me the old air turns. It turns
beside our instruments.
A mind in its child parts.
Even today the day threatens
to grow into itself
until tomorrow hears it.

JOHN GALLAHER

Why Dessert Is More Memorable Than Dinner

At what age is it when we realize we know much about diminished things? I want it to be a real age. A real answer. And I don't want it to be "diminished things," either. I want a list. I don't want it to be "different for everyone." I want it to be something like "By age 40 one knows much of *this*, *this*, and *this*." All the thises there are. A unity of experience that forms a layer of solace over the truth of diminished things, a way to say that I'm now 40 and I have passed through the veil. But it keeps not happening. It's veils all the way down. "Just remember, Duckies," the ineffable says, "everybody gets in rows." And that, what, is supposed to be a version of answer. The diminished answer, and possibly by age 40, apparent. It says we have this common experience, misery's company, but for most of us, it's just company, a world of company, where I (or we, if I'm feeling community-minded) want more stories of going to the supermarket, buying something, then going home unmolested. Stories with beginnings, middles, and ends, and all three a version where nothing inevitable happens, nothing irrevocable. I want to call that "hope for the future," a glorious hopefulness of orthodontist appointments, soccer practice (4:15–5:30 Tuesdays and Thursdays), the unremarkable futurity of events. Bricks. The promise of a brick, solid. And then a wall. And with this wall, I want color, bright, impossible color. Jolly Rancher Green, Jolly Rancher Red . . . because color is happiness. It's "first day," steeping in it and knowing it. I know it. Like the brand new smell of getting to the future a bit ahead of everyone else that was the climax of that Steven King story where somehow this airliner got off the track of the present, or like the conversations I have with the kids about Ugli fruit, the orange/grapefruit exotic unknown from another world, because when else was it, really, that any of us was at our most, what? Our most something. Anything. I spend a lot of time asking that. And I really would like to know. I'd sit with each one of you and ask, and then have follow-up questions. I'm sure I'd have follow-up questions, as for each "glorious hopefulness" contender, each best, happiest, there's always some fundamental thing that hasn't figured in yet, or has figured in differently than we think, where you miscounted the car sales for the month or the milk order, all of which goes into the mix of phrases like "I didn't know it then, but that was the best time in my life." So if you were back there again, you'd need to bring all the rest of your experiences with you, and if you did that, nostalgia would drown you. I'd hate to see that happen to the most hopeful time in my life, when we were at our best, living in that bright white house, standing in the full sun on the back porch, with coffee.

There's Desolation, True,
but What If It's *Magnificent* Desolation?

We're playing the "Getting to Know You" game, and it's going
to take the rest of our lives. The cards all start with something
along the lines of "I'm the kind of person who . . ." and "What
would you do if . . ." So here we are with the card of cards, The Fool,
who asks, "What did your first love smell like?" And I'm ready
to run through a plate glass window to get away, which is level two
in the "Getting to Know You" game, the getting to know myself level,
the Please Get Me The Hell Out Of Here level. My first love smelled
like Prell shampoo, though I've no idea who my first love was. Maybe
it's in how you define love. Is it kissing after school in the empty
waiting room of the guidance counselor's office? Or, better, is it when
you're five, and it's this stuffed bear you sleep with every night? Why not
love the bear, who smelled like carpet and faintly musty? My favorite bear
saved my life once, when I fell off the top bunk at a cousin's house.
It was a big bear, and why not call it my first love, why not reserve
the first for one who saves your life? Save my life and I'll love you
forever, or at least until I rationalize my way out of it, which is probably
more the case. I haven't had much opportunity to test the theory out
after the bear. I should have called it Savior Bear, but I didn't. At least
I'm pretty sure I didn't, as I've no idea what I named that bear, probably
Beary McBear, or something. Truth is I don't think of that bear at all.
It just came to me now, in this context. Love at first memory, then
they go away, these saviors, these loves, who were so important for
a time that some of us kill ourselves over them. There's my high school
classmate who played drums and hung himself one night over them,
supposedly over love. I've thought about that a lot. And then the next
thought, that they (his parents, probably) had to do something with those
drums. They had to be given away or sold. Love, they say, is in the nose,
from birth all the way through, as continually new research about
our sensory systems arrives, showing that the nose is central to the way
we form relationships. I'll think about that a little bit, as a kind of
desolation, I suppose, though I originally thought I'd say "consolation,"
I even started to write it, but among the hallucinations that trouble me
most are these desperate moments that come with the scent of Prell,

the familiar, stop-you-in-your-tracks moments where I'm left having
to walk away, when I don't want to walk away. I want to drown
in Prell. I want to throw myself from a bunk bed at night into a depthless
slowing universe of people and things that hold you and don't go.

MIGUEL MURPHY

Amateur

A warm carcass
like a handcuff, the whole
thing emptying, & darkening
on my wrist. Feeling

around what—a sack, a body-
bag, ghastly, the warped
gigantic asshole of a calf
on a farm. He's sick, I think,

reaching up.
Maybe the dark moon-
light on my hands later
will make sense. My curious

disappearing.
That warble of flesh. It's
the view, the drowned
from the bottom of

non-being. I want to be
alive, but I don't under-
stand why. The camera
hand joins in and

we pull out the drugged
kid's wet intestines
while he shakes his head
on all fours and passes

out moaning in some
realm not framed in this
gleaming bright whitening
landscape of slop.

Let him sleep it off
at the Ramada on Sunset.
Watch it. Weird meat,
my muse, I'm trying to help.

MICHAEL BAZZETT

The Taxidermist & the Cloud

The taxidermist looked at the creamy musculature of cumulus

outlined against the blue.
                     Only the thick stuff from the top,
he murmured. And so crisp in this light.

Then he inquired: How would you like to be this way forever?

The cloud had yet to hold a pose for even
the slenderest moment, allowing the slow churn of air to turn
        it always into something

else.   I've got rain in the belly and thoughts of roiling
                   up into the body of a thunderhead
before toppling back down in a fine-haired mizzle, said the cloud.

But I could capture you from the best angle
                 and make you beautiful
forever, said the taxidermist.
        And how long would that be? asked the cloud.

Longer than you can remember in both directions,
                 said the taxidermist.
The cloud sighed. I can only always remember myself
      as water through and in the above and the drenching

deep into the soil until bearded roots pull me through green
                   bodies into sky.
        I am both verb and ocean.

That's not a bad little speech,
        said the taxidermist, lighting a cigarette.

He inhaled the smoke hungrily through his nose like a wolf
                              and sent a miniature
cloud from his throat. Very funny,

said the cloud.   A strange odor hovered in the air, like singed tin,
                              before the crackling bolt struck.

Translation Folio

JAN WAGNER

Translator's Introduction

David Keplinger

JAN WAGNER HAS PUBLISHED SEVEN books in his native Germany, won several prizes, translates American poets widely (among them Charles Simic, a likely pairing), travels the world reading his poetry, which has been translated into numerous languages, yet he remains unknown to English-speaking audiences, despite having translators currently toiling in Ireland, Canada, and America. More wildly apparent is the fact that his poetry—difficult because it is layered with metrical forms, rhyme, alliteration, syllabics, and references to myth and legend—is so impeccably crafted in the German, the translator in any tongue must concede that theirs is an art of roundings off at best. As translator, and as reader, this is work you have to wrestle.

Wagner and I have been wrestling with his sound and sense for more than five years, and, if you too are a poet engaged in the art of literary translation, you understand the sorrow-joy or joy-sorrow that goes into the craft. You begin to think like this language you don't really speak (as I speak no German, though I am called its "translator"). You begin to describe it in kennings calling back the shared, Anglo-Saxon roots. You begin to say "joy-sorrow" as if it is actually something (and it is) and you celebrate (as we have done) the unexpected ring of "koi" with "coin" in English, that is, the ways the poem actually becomes in the new language a new work, neither mine nor his but ours. In our pages and pages of notes for each poem, Wagner and I have been as two men attempting to balance a dime on its rim, each using one finger. In the last drafts of the poem, we are barely touching it, and the dime stays standing on its side.

In my past attempts as translator, I worked in the Danish (*World Cut Out with Crooked Scissors: the Selected Poetry of Carsten Rene Nielsen*, and again from Nielsen, *House Inspections*). Nielsen is a prose poet; the problem in his case was untangling the idiomatic expressions and the timing—the dark humor—of his poetry, and then deciding which of the hundreds of pieces we've translated carries over. And there's a rhythm to Nielsen's prose poems, too; something dactyllic and falling down in the sentences, and a staggered quality that has to do with sentence length. These were liberally manipulated and reinvented to satisfy the demands of English semantics. In Wagner, the whole game had to be re-invented. Here, as in "kyrnica morska," you have sapphics; and in "rain barrel variations" a series of haikus. In both cases, as with all the poetry, the strict form could not be sacrificed for the sake of the sense. (It's not just something poets say.) The sense was being carried in the form.

It's all rather like the image of a rat floating in the rain barrel in "rain barrel variations," the poem which became the title piece for Wagner's latest collection in Germany. He writes of the moment the boy lifts the lid of the barrel, discovering the animal inside, "what got imprinted / in me, framed in the barrel, / like a locket: rat." Each of these poems hangs as locket with that hard exterior, which, if it's working well, clicks right open, snaps quickly shut. Instead of the face of the lover inside, a rat. A dead rat. There's something spookily Grimm's about it all. The psychological effect is the same as what we experienced in childhood, first time we lost ourselves inside a horror story. The music delights us, and we let go: and so the image drives more deeply in.

JAN WAGNER : Five Poems

sloes

what was so blue like evenings in the fall
or black like the bible? what hung, was so harsh,
through mist-smoke, october-showers, so whole-
ly bitter that everything contracted? the sloe.

we moved towards them after the first frost
at the forest edge—in-the-rough barbarians,
entrenched behind the thorns, and iced
on the ground, where we kneeled for the berries

to grope for their tender and damas-
ken skin, to cautiously grasp at the interior,
to search the inside like a doubting thomas
asks questions, and there was time to wonder,

to think of other things—of osmosis,
the next class test, nylon stockings,
of nina wriggers' breasts and of the cosmos,
which at some point in the near future its border,
       its point of greatest possible extension,
       would reach and shrink,

starting with the sky, with the country, school
and city, with us ourselves, until the whole world
upon nothing but a twiglet would hang: sloe.
no wonder, how heavy the buckets were, filled

with deepest blue. behind us the bushes—
a text, almost devoid of vowels, its words
a thicket, a bunch of tangled pen-scratches.
the rest of it we left there to the birds.

from the globe factory

once, i set down my breaktime-bread
in the yet-to-be constructed portions
of the southern hemisphere. some child
now picks his nose there, seeking the sandwich islands.

it was a perfect world. with colors, zones
and forty watts as center point;
no wars and no secessions,
only the slight odor of dissolvent.

at night the trucks abandon us to silence
in the hall, and they deliver in light cartons
the cosmos to the windows of the children,
that round, blue radiance;

we however earn the next day's wages
in eternal neon again, one as atlas,
another as a solar eclipse, demiurges
in work coats, deities with overalls.

it's often that i dream of the equator
as a line which one could follow
through the forests, continents, low-
lands, a precise frontier: every bird

becomes two birds, one before
and one behind the line, all things there
are segregated, day from night, north
from south. winter stares at summer.

every cloud is two clouds, a snow-
ball lands as a puddle. the mountainside
halts, becomes a plain, the tiny pond
loses its name. on the left rises smoke

from the baker's, on the right the butcher
whets the knives—and the lovers
wave once more to each other, as he goes
from his house, and at hers the shutters close.

koalas

so much sleep in only one tree,
so many gray globes
of fur in all the branches, a bohemia
of sluggishness which itself in the treetops holds and holds

and holds with a couple of crampons
as claws. nor was it ever credited, first to take
the journey above the whistling fans
of rainforest canopy, ruffled stoics,

shoddy buddhas, tougher than the poison
in the leaves, with their cotton-wool-
ears against enticements, immune
in some cranny of the world: no waterloo

for them, no walk to canossa.
take note of them, memorize them
while there is time—this face in repose,
this expression of a cyclist

very close to stage win, dis-
connected from the ground, but within our reach
in jaded gray, before each of them yawns, stretches,
drops off into a dream of eucalyptus.

krynica morska

vodka from five countries, in seven pallid
bellies swaying, gurgling, andrzej. we passed it
all around the room and we raised the bottles:
        vodka as fanfare.

night: a moored balloon which at its rain-ropes
tore; an august thunderstorm that trekked from
way up north and over the sea, and trekked to
        krynica morska,

to the beach, rimantas, and to the clothes-heaps,
tossed to peaceful animals: every lightning
strike ripped darkness off us, and so we stood there
        naked as a tribe,

only now discovered. and we ran, ilya,
slammed the waves behind us, and we drifted
there between the black and blacker, halina,
        mikhel, and smuggled

all that high-grade stuff through surf, just as
concurrently, beneath the lights all tinkling
the free-for-all back in the bar poseidon
        began without us.

rain barrel variations

i lifted the lid
and stared into the giant
eye of the blackbird.

•

beneath the plum tree
behind the house, unmoved, cool
like a zen master.

•

a sort of oven
in negative, without smoke,
gulping up the clouds.

•

gurgled just a bit,
if you bashed hard against it,
but disclosed nothing.

•

as if the dead climbed
through her from the netherworld,
to listen to us.

•

silvery organ-
pipe, squat gutterspout: through which
pumped all the weather.

•

one summer long
fully sated. then, with storm,
it bubbled over.

•

stay, spoke that darkness,
and your face dissolves itself
like a sugar lump.

•

old as the garden,
redolent as forest-lake.
there: barrel of styx.

•

i lifted the lid,
twitched back. the blackbird singing
suddenly darkened.

•

awash in autumn,
it leaked out by the hundreds
the heaps of black slugs.

•

what got imprinted
in me, framed in the barrel,
like a locket: *rat.*

•

last drop from the tree.
in the quiet, quietly,
the quivering gong.

•

a brooding, brooding;
in winter, enlightenment
as a disc of ice.

Translated from the German by David Keplinger

KATE McINTYRE

The Moat

1

IN VERN AND DELLA'S EIGHTH year of marriage, in early March, Vern lost his job as demolition technician at the limestone quarry. After the supervisor told him, he scooped up his hardhat, thermos, lunch pail, and harness, cussing and kicking his way out to his truck. He found Della at home in the kitchen cooking a batch of jam. Della took one look at him, dusty and hangdog, stubbly and limp-armed, and knew the other shoe had dropped.

"Those idiots at A & B finally let me go," he told her. She supposed she should have let him lay his head on her breasts while she ran her fingers through his wispy blond hair, but she had just added the pectin. The jam required constant stirring at this delicate stage. Also, Vern deserved it. He'd bragged about how he'd kicked the supervisor's shed each time he walked past and dropped pinches of quarry grit into the other workers' lunch pails. When he told her these things she'd nodded in sympathy. Vern wasn't the sort of man you questioned.

"What am I going to do now?" Vern asked. He stood with his hands on his hips, his lower lip puffed out the way their son Harland did his when he was frustrated. Della shook her head and eyed the bubbling jam. The quarry was all Vern knew.

They had met at the quarry. She had worked in the shed watching the men break rock. The supervisor said the men who did Vern's job were either the dumbest or the bravest. Della had thought Vern was the bravest.

When she got pregnant, Vern made her quit. She didn't want to, but he said he'd take care of her, and at nineteen, she found that beautiful. Maybe if she'd still been there, she could have kept an eye on him and they'd have two paychecks rather than zero.

The jam was ready to pour, but Della kept stirring. Vern's eyes flicked at her, daring her to say something. Silently, Della stirred. She'd had this same feeling on her wedding day—another matter Vern had sullied. It was a fury too big to be contained in her body. If she spoke now, her voice would come out quadruple bass. Her words would blow Vern's hair back and send him sprawling out of her kitchen so she could pour her damn jam before it spoiled. She didn't speak. Vern wandered out.

She made a mental list of all of the good things about Vern: he didn't have problems with alcohol, he never beat the children, he didn't waste money at the dog park or speedway, he used to be very attractive, he was the only family she had left besides the boys now that her dad was gone. Della's father hadn't liked Vern. He said that once you stripped away the pale hair, flayed the sunburnt skin, teased off the stringy muscle, all that remained was fear. Della had said that was true of everyone she knew.

2

DELLA AND VERN AND THEIR boys Harland and Mylan lived on Old Highway 40, after the town petered out to squat, rambling country houses, and after the country houses themselves thinned. They had a seven-room ranch house and detached garage on five acres. Vern had built the garage. It leaned. The nearest house was a couple miles away, not even in shouting distance.

Vern spent hours outside now, digging weeds from the deep green, close-cropped lawn using an icepick in their wedding pattern. Their bank balance sloughed away, but he refused to look for another job. Della tried to help him, but nothing suited. He'd shake his head as Della read ads from the employment section of the *Salina Journal*: carpet shampooer, light duty lube technician, over-the-road flatbed driver.

Finally he applied for seasonal work as a silo washer (dangling three stories, volatile wheat particles blowing up his nose, the power sprayer vibrating away thoughts—just up Vern's alley, Della reckoned), but they said he was too old.

Vern read the paper, too, though he was more interested in the crime blotter than the help-wanteds.

Della was returning from a jam delivery in town one day when Vern waved her over to the lawn. Sheets of newspaper and limp weeds ringed him, sending up a sharp green odor and the old tire smell of ink. "A woman was raped in town this week. Also, somebody broke into a truck and stole the stereo. I sure would miss my stereo," he told her, pointing the icepick. He picked dirt off the grape design in the handle.

"That poor woman," Della said. "Have they found the man that did it?"

"Nope, they haven't. Yet another reason you shouldn't be getting over to Salina alone. You're too cute," he told her. "And not very strong."

Della objected to that last bit. She'd been hoisting jam pots long enough that her arm muscles stood out. But Vern was underfoot so much now, and there was so very much jam to make and only so much time in the day that she said, "Maybe you could do a few deliveries. Get out of the house, see some folks. Someone might even have a lead on a job."

Vern grunted.

Della told him, "Well, you don't have to look for work right now. I'll be your jam-making sugar mama." She could up her production to three, four hundred jars a week. Maybe put it in smaller jars. The folks who bought her jam at her friend

Crystal's store were passing it on—gifts for neighbors, pastors, mailmen. Crystal said they weren't looking for a good price per ounce, but a nice presentation. Maybe she was right.

"How are you going to take care of the kids when you're swanning off to town every other minute?" Vern said.

Lately Della felt like she was dealing less with a man than with a sick animal. Better just to let it crawl in a corner and lick its wounds. The boys were fine.

But Della couldn't help herself. "What's the problem now?"

"I'm sad, Della. I ain't got no purpose anymore," Vern said. "The supervisor said I was good for nothing and he knew I had been since the day he hired me. Twelve years and he says that."

"Oh, Vern," Della said. She grasped his shoulder. He shrugged her off.

"I don't need sympathy. I just thought that was real crappy."

He did this often, pissed her off then made her feel sorry for him. It worked, even though she could see it coming from a mile off.

Della said, "You've taken care of us for such a long time, is all I'm saying. Everyone deserves a break."

3

In May, two months after Vern lost his job, Della ladled jam into sterilized jars and Vern stood over her asking if she hadn't perhaps overcooked this batch. The boys arrived home from school and peered in the kitchen warily. Lately Vern had turned affectionate, scooping them up and hugging too hard. If they saw him, they bolted. She wished she were as agile. Today she told them to come in. They were a couple of round, solid boys, tow-headed like their daddy. They wore puffy coats in the winter, a Chiefs one for Harland, and a camouflage print for Mylan. In the summer, they wore T-shirts printed with robots or eagles and American flags and shorts with elasticized waists. Their eyelids didn't even have creases yet. She squatted to hug them, burrowing her nose deep in Mylan's hair, which smelled of sweet grass and baby shampoo. She asked how their day had gone, and Harland told her, "I've got to build a diorama. A castle."

"Well," Della said, "That sounds like something your father could help with. He's always been so handy with building things. What do you say, Vern?"

Vern was always awkward with affection. He stood a few feet away. "Yep, son. I reckon I could help you out." Della's shoulders relaxed. "Let's go take a browse in them encyclopedias while your mother gets dinner on the table." The boys and their father trooped down to the basement to dig out the "C" from a 1981 *World Book Encyclopedia* set, inherited from Vern's uncle.

They stormed the stairs when Della called them to dinner, abuzz with talk of turrets and battlements and lances and trebuchets (also known as catapults, they told her), and bows and arrows and chain mail and towers. And moats.

Vern, breathing hard from the climb, pointed at Della. "She's our queen," he announced to the boys. "I'm the king and you two are knights gallant."

Harland looked at Mylan and said, "I think he should be the squire." Their father laughed and punched Harland on the shoulder. Harland jumped, his eyes welling up.

"Right, and our house is our castle," Della said quickly, rolling her eyes but smiling to make sure Vern knew she was just kidding.

"Yep," Vern said, "the house is my castle."

"I'm glad to see you all are making progress." Della told the boys, "I'm thinking about making a big batch of apple butter after school tomorrow, and I need a couple strong men to help me. Do you know of anyone who might be available?"

The boys looked at each other, then at Vern. "I don't know," Harlan said. "Maybe."

"Maybe, huh? You got plans?" Della asked.

Harlan looked up at Vern again. Vern winked.

4

DELLA NOTICED THAT VERN SLEPT strangely well that night. He didn't move enough during the day so at night he usually thrashed. When he came in the kitchen the next morning, Della asked if he'd like some coffee. He said yes, after he woke up the boys. He smiled. He never smiled or offered to wake up the boys. Lately, he didn't wake up before the boys left for school.

Della could hear Harland and Mylan giggling in their room, Vern's voice deep and muddled. She suspected they were planning some fun she would usually object to—a trip to the rodeo, or a demolition derby, maybe.

All three of them ran into the kitchen. The boys smiled up at her like they had a secret they were dying to spill. Vern said, "Now, we can't jump the gun on something like this. Lady of the house has final say." Della passed bacon and eggs and ketchup and leftover fried chicken.

Plate filled, Vern turned to Della. He said, "I'm gonna dig a moat all around you. 'Cause my house is my castle, and you are my queen. I'm not going to stop with this one, though. You know how we've always talked about starting our own business?"

"A moat? Like medieval times? Why would anyone want that in their yard?" Had this terrible idea spiraled his brain while he'd rested so meekly last night? She wanted to laugh but he looked so serious. And besides, they already had Della's Delectables, her jam business.

"Vern's Moats, we'll call it. I'll take commissions from people who want moats around their own yards. We'll build one here first to let everybody see what we can do. It'll be a show moat. We'll put some signs on the highway: Come see the Show Moat, and find out how to get your own."

He told her that demand would be huge, especially around Valentine's Day, though the frozen ground might present excavation problems. He already knew the basics from his time at the quarry. He even had ideas for mini-moats for doghouses. He figured that everyone in the county would be clamoring for one for aesthetic and security reasons. "They're romantic, too, as I said about the queen stuff. A moat fit for a queen in her castle. We could sell lawn ornaments, too, that look like monsters or crocodiles. Moat ornaments, I guess they'd be."

"My," Della said. They studied her face.

"I knew she wouldn't like it, boys," Vern snapped. "She can have her own business but God forbid anyone else tries to do something for this family." The boys turned their eyes to the floor. Mylan sighed hard.

"I didn't mean I didn't like it," Della said, half for the boys, half for how it might give Vern something to do so he wasn't underfoot and paranoid. "Maybe this would be just the thing. You and the boys could work on it together."

Vern had risen half out of his seat still grasping a chicken leg, his thigh muscles tense. Now he settled back, picked the bone clean with his teeth, and tossed it plateward.

Harland asked, "Are you going to use C4 to make the moat?"

"Nah, son, we aren't going down but ten feet or so. Not as far as the substrate. Though if we did, we'd have no need for the garden hose for water. Eventually, we'd hit the water table, and the thing would fill up like a big old well. Wouldn't that be something?"

"I'm sure you know what you're doing," Della said. But she wasn't, and Vern was moving way too fast. He'd trapped her using the boys as bait.

"Yep, the only thing I regret is that it won't be done in time to be an anniversary present." Vern kicked back in his chair and scratched his belly.

5

FROM WHAT DELLA COULD TELL from the kitchen window during the next week, moat planning involved Vern getting drunk. He'd drain a six-pack of cheap beer and pace his yard with new clarity.

He'd head inside panting, grab Della, and tell her things. Once he said that he saw the problem with his plot of land, and with Kansas in general: "The ground is too level around the house. There's no trees to speak of. Everybody who takes half a glance from the road can see our whole spread crystal-clear."

"I don't see why that's such a problem," Della said.

"But what if you're out front tending the garden, all bent over in your shorts, them riding up your legs, and some pervert spots you."

"I don't find that very likely, Vern. Only four or five cars pass on any given day."

"It only takes one," Vern said, low and foreboding, yet still smiling. "One to park a half mile up the road and sneak back after dark with a big knife, and rape you and make the boys watch and slice them up, all before I had the chance to fight back."

"Nobody'd rape or slice you, though, huh?"

"Nope," Vern said.

6

ONE NIGHT DELLA SAT DOWN beside Vern on the couch and told him how Harland and Mylan were outgrowing their clothes. Harland couldn't bend his elbows in his jacket, it stretched so tight on his back, and Mylan's elastic-waist shorts cut his belly skin.

"We need money, Vern, to buy the boys things," Della said, "And my jam can only do so much."

Vern said, "You remember Hank at that Mobile station on Crawford? He told me a while ago that they needed more guys. In a week or two, I'll talk to him. Just 'til I get the moats going, though. That's the real plan." He sighed, hitched his pants up, and pulled her down onto his lap. His belt buckle dug into her side. She was glad he was laying off the moat. Maybe he'd forget entirely, like he had the nightcrawler business or the sub sandwich franchise.

"Whose wife are you, sweetheart?" Vern asked.

"Yours, honey."

"Mine and only mine?"

"Yes. Yours and only yours." They had played this game when they first got married, when words like "wife," "husband," and "our flatware pattern" still sounded exciting, when Della was still caught up in that intermingled grief at losing her father and delight at finding Vern—so strong, so handsome, so handy on the scene.

He kissed her and slid his square hand along the waistband of her sweatpants. When he started fumbling with the drawstring, Della's mind raced for an excuse. He had been so amorous lately. He used to come home from the quarry too exhausted to think about anything except soaking up TV and a High Life. Now, he was, "Ready to eat a piece of her, she looked so tasty."

Vern held her with his fingers laced around her back. She had a double batch of blueberry bubbling on the stove, and she could just picture it boiling over on her white Formica countertop. She slid to her feet.

"Don't be a tease." Vern said. He let her go.

7

BETWEEN BATCHES OF JAM, DELLA watched Vern and the boys from the kitchen window. Vern would bring a load of limestone from the quarry, the truck riding low with the weight of the smooth, buff-colored slabs. School ended in late May, so Vern and the boys spent whole days outside. They used shovels to dig a trench around the perimeter of the manicured grass. She couldn't invite her friends and the neighbors over because Vern and the boys had created such an eyesore, but then again, friends and neighbors had rarely visited before. They didn't exactly live on the main drag. Their house wasn't the sort of place where people just popped in. Unless they were perverts, if Vern was right. Which he wasn't.

One day, Vern rumbled up in a backhoe. Della prayed it was just rented. Grinding gears accompanied Della's jam-making for the next few days, and the moat grew much quicker. Dust from the excavation blew through the cracks in the windows, and she had to be vigilant to keep it from tainting her batches.

A couple days later, Della was picking the first strawberries of the summer from her little garden plot and stowing them in her apron when she glanced at the construction. Vern and Harland were standing around in hard hats while the backhoe bit chunks out of their yard. But if Vern was not operating the backhoe, who was? Della ran to them, shielding her eyes from the sun as she looked up and saw Mylan's head, barely visible over the steering wheel.

"Why is Mylan running the backhoe?" she asked.

Vern said, "Settle down now, Della, Mylan's plenty old enough to run a backhoe. You should be proud of him, the way he handles that double clutch." The bucket paused at the top of its arc like a beckoning finger.

"Come down, baby," Della called. She could only raise one arm to Mylan—the other held the berries in her apron. "Nice and slow." She almost grasped his foot.

Mylan shook his head. "No way, Warty," he yelled. He kicked her hand away. Lately, Vern called her "Little Mrs. Worrywart." Mylan and Harland picked it up and started calling her Worrywart or Miss Wart or just Warty.

"Hey now," Vern said.

Mylan straightened right up.

"Apologize to your mother."

"I'm sorry," Mylan said. "Do I have to get off?" he asked Vern.

"Nah, that's okay, son."

Mylan and Harlan seemed to have forgotten all about how Vern would rip limbs off action figures that didn't get put away as he'd asked, how Della was the one who cuddled them and told them Vern didn't mean anything by it, he just had a temper.

"You go on back into your kitchen now," Vern said.

Della slunk back to the house, closing the door on Vern yelling, "Woo-boy, son! Get it." She could just imagine that Mylan'd get the gearshift confused and bring that heavy shovel part down on his brother's head. Then she had a thought, an evil thought. Which was if Mylan brought the shovel down on Vern's head they could bury him in the moat and pretend he'd never happened. When she opened her apron, the strawberries were smashed. She rinsed them in her colander and threw them in her pot, her hands twitching wildly.

8

A FEW DAYS LATER, DELLA asked if she could take the truck and do the jam delivery because she hadn't been to town in such a long time. Vern had been running her jams in and picking up new jars and supplies for the past month, and she missed her chats with Crystal. In fact, she realized she hadn't seen anybody but Vern and the boys for weeks.

Vern said, "I'm using limestone rather than brick to edge the moat. Limestone is craggier than brick. Lots of people don't think about that. It affects the way you mix the concrete. I make mine smoother."

"Honey, you didn't hear me. Could I have the truck for an hour or so?"

"The truck? Nah, I don't think so."

Della waited for his explanation, but it never came.

"The truck, Vern. I'm taking it."

"I don't think so," he said. "The carburetor's been real funny on that truck, and I'm the only one who knows how to tweak it."

"Sometimes I get the feeling you don't want me to leave the house."

"Now why would you think that? Though the boys and I do miss you terribly when you're gone. You're the heart of our home, Della."

The heart. Della liked that.

9

THE NEXT DAY, AN ETCHED limestone sign appeared in the yard. "For Della," it said. Vern told her, "Del, this moat is like my Taj Mahal, just for you."

Della asked, "Wasn't the wife of the man who built the Taj Mahal dead?"

"Yep," Vern replied. He pointed out how there was room at the top of the plaque for more engraving, and that "In Memoriam" could be added easily, along with applicable dates, God forbid.

Vern cut their phone service. He explained that because of moat cost overruns, they couldn't afford a regular phone anymore. He had gotten a pre-paid cell, though, which he kept on a holder on his belt loop. He told her just let him know whenever she wanted to call anyone. She asked him once if she could borrow it to call Crystal, but he said he was waiting for an important business call, and besides, the phone was out of batteries. He and the boys communicated across the yard using walkie-talkies. The boys thought it was funny to make farting noises into the walkie-talkie and yell, "Excuse me!" Della thought it was kind of funny, too, but Vern didn't. He said they should respect their equipment.

Something funny was happening with Crystal. Vern brought back less and less money from the jam. There was only $25 from the last batch. This made no sense, because she always asked Vern how many jars Crystal wanted, and he always said, "Same as last week." What was she doing with all that extra jam, if she wasn't selling it?

She'd asked Vern about it. He told her something about Crystal doing a new mail order business so she needed a bigger inventory. It hadn't made a lot of sense

The concrete bottom of the moat was poured in mid-June. Once it dried, Vern built up the inner walls using limestone chunks. He told his sons, "Men, we're protecting the house from bad guys. Make these walls real thick, okay, so that nobody's going to sneak in and get to your mother." The boys hopped up and down in their little tan steel-toed boots and added extra smears of concrete with their child-size trowels. Neither of them kissed their mother goodnight any more. They ducked their heads and pretended to be asleep when she went to tuck them in. Probably just a phase. They'd been mama's boys for so long that it was high time Vern got a turn.

10

On July 4th, the moat was ready. Vern decided that a ceremony was in order. He and the boys wore their suits, and Vern insisted that Della put on a nice dress. Mylan had just started playing the trumpet with the school band. He could play taps or "Twinkle, Twinkle, Little Star," so Vern had him play taps because it better matched the gravity of the occasion. Vern ran a large-nozzled pump and hose unit from their well over to the empty moat and sent Harland around with a monkey wrench making sure the couplings were tight. As Mylan sputtered away on trumpet, Vern opened a spigot, and the first rush of water splashed the moat floor. The family watched the puddle spread until it became clear that the moat would not appear before their very eyes. It took a week to fill.

Just as the water finally lapped the top edge of the limestone, Della tried sneaking past Vern with her boxes of jam. Somehow she was nervous, though she'd told herself it would just be a fun surprise for Vern when she got back. Save him a trip. She looked over her shoulder as she got them all loaded in the truck. As she slid the keys into the ignition, Vern appeared at the driver's side window. Della jumped. He peered into the cab, his eyes moving over every inch of her and the upholstery.

"Vern," Della said, putting a hand over her chest to conceal the pounding of her heart. "I was thinking I'd take the truck out for a little spin, go on down to the store. I'm getting stir-crazy in this place."

Silence.

Then Vern said, "You said you were headed out with the jam? Tell you what, let me take it in for you. I'm going to town anyway to get an estimate on some ten-foot pikes." He opened the door. Della stayed a moment, her fingers clasping the steering wheel. Vern lifted her hands away and set them in her lap. He slid her across the vinyl seat and out, onto the road. "Easy, there," he told her.

When Vern returned with the pikes (the estimate had been reasonable), it was twilight. Della had been sitting on a lawn chair for several hours, looking out at the moat. She had a terrible feeling that if she didn't get away now, she never would, and the boys never would. An image came to her, one that she'd call up often in times of difficulty. She lay on her deathbed. A rustic quilt covered her. Her heavily tendoned, liver-spotted hands lay in her sons' hands, Harland's hard from working the land, and Mylan's soft from his study of business, the knowledge he'd gained at college turning Della and him into a real Ms. and Mr. Smuckers. The boys' voices would join in reedy harmony. "We love you, mother," they'd say, as she drifted toward eternal repose. And where was Vern? Vern was ever absent, dead and buried somewhere, or not. Blown to bits, most likely, and scattered through the quarry—a bloody stump, a dab of viscera, a spatter of blood over the quarry rock. But Vern had bucked that plan. He looked to be the survivor in the current scenario. She asked, "Why aren't you showing the moat to anyone yet, now that it's done?"

Vern sat down on the swing beside her, draping an arm across the back of her neck. "I don't really want to bring loads of people over here to see it. That would defeat the whole purpose, don't you think?"

"I thought the purpose was making some money."

"Sweetheart. The world's too dangerous for us to go out there and deal with people like that. You're staying right here with me forever, ok?" He stroked her cheek with the backs of his sandpapery fingers. Della went inside and shut the door. Nothing bad was happening here. Not in her little house. She just had to keep her wits about her. The way bad things worked was they snuck up on you. One false step on a quarry ledge, just when your footing felt sure.

11

THE NEXT DAY DAWNED CLEAR and cool. Della opened the kitchen window to pick up the breeze. The moat wasn't looking so bad now that the heavy equipment was gone. Vern had set the limestone perfectly level, she could say that for him. Maybe once the moat was done, she and the boys could get a fossil guide book and try to identify the creatures that had died in the limestone centuries ago. Or they could have a big party for her upcoming birthday. Show Crystal and her husband and the boys' friends the monstrosity. She overheard Harland and Vern standing in the shade of the house talking. Harland said, "Dad, Crystal came by again. I told her Mom wasn't home."

"Good job, son. It's important that we keep the outsiders away."

Della stepped back from the window, feeling cold despite the kitchen's heat. After ten minutes, she nearly had herself convinced that the conversation she had overheard never happened. What she had really heard was that Harland had called Crystal on the telephone, but she wasn't home. They were probably planning a surprise party for her birthday, and of course Crystal would be invited. Also, a finger of land wide enough to drive the truck across remained. The moat was not yet impregnable. She told herself these things and didn't believe them.

When Vern came in for lunch, she asked him, "What's up with that one little spit of land on the moat?" Her voice was even. Vern didn't know she knew about Crystal. She'd been hiding her emotions from Vern for so long that it was no challenge now.

"Oh, right beside the guard tower? That's where the drawbridge will go, honey. Yep, that will be gone by tomorrow. We're going to knock it out with the bulldozer. We've finally got all the supplies collected on this side of the moat, so we don't need it anymore. There'll be a password for the drawbridge," he added.

"Oh, that's fun. Do I get to help choose?"

Vern looked away for a moment, his face pained, and said, "The boys and I talked about this, Dell, and we've decided that it's best if you don't know it. You're our weak link, physically, and someone could, God forbid, use force to get it from you. It would compromise the integrity of our compound."

Della found her unsold jam when she went to look for more jars in the garage after dinner. Boxes stacked on boxes, the pink of the strawberry, the deep magenta of the mulberry, the cerise of the rose hip, all her work, weeks of it, there in one place. It was awe-inspiring, really, how much she'd done, and she gave herself a moment to appreciate it. The boxes were stacked roughly, and a sour cherry batch had broken on the concrete. Wasps buzzed the sharded jars, their flight paths crazy, their wings slow from the sugar.

12

DELLA LAY SLEEPLESS BESIDE VERN that night. When had he gone around the bend, sanity-wise? Where had he even learned about things like the "integrity of the compound?" She and the boys would be trapped tomorrow. She struggled and struggled, but she kept coming back to one conclusion—the only conclusion: she couldn't be in that house come morning, and neither could the boys. She would spirit them away, and then, she and Vern could sort everything out once they'd all gotten some distance on things, physically and emotionally. And by sorting she meant divorce. Obviously she couldn't get any distance while she was surrounded by the moat.

Della tried three times to get out of bed. Each time she eased herself upright, she heard Vern stir, so she settled back on the mattress, making sure that her breathing was slow and regular. On her fourth try, Vern didn't move a muscle.

She crept to Vern's side of the bed, grabbed his keys from the night table, and ran, her pink nightgown flapping her thighs. She scooped Mylan out of bed, but found Harland's bed empty. She dashed through the house carrying Mylan, searching each room for her lost boy. She went outside, but he wasn't there, either. Finally, she shook Mylan gently and asked him, "Where's your brother, honey? Where's Harland?"

"In the guard tower," he mumbled.

She looked up. Vern and the boys had built the guard tower the previous week. It was fifteen feet tall with a roofed hut on top. Sure enough, Harland peered down. He wore camouflage hunting pants and held an air rifle.

Della said through ragged breaths, "Come on down, honey. We're going to get on out of here for a while. Just you boys and me. A real trip."

Harland stepped away from the railing. He returned with a walkie-talkie. "Daddy said you might try this," he told her. He spoke into the walkie-talkie, "Big Eagle, Big Eagle, come in. This is Little Eagle One. She's trying to get away."

There was a long pause. Then the crackling reply, "I'll be right out, soldier." As Della gazed up at Harland, she loosened her grip on Mylan. He wriggled away and climbed to his brother.

She yelled up, "Come on guys. We can get ice cream. You don't want me to go without you, do you?" She took a half step toward the truck.

They stared down at her.

"Please, honey? Mylan? Last one to the pick-up's a rotten egg."

Mylan chewed his fingers and Harland played with the walkie-talkie. Della scanned the yard for Vern. Still no sign.

"Hey there boys, I'll take you to the Wal-Mart. It's open twenty-four hours. You can have as many toys as you can carry. What do you say?"

Harland set his air rifle on the railing and brought his eye to the sight.

"Now, Harland, you stop that right now," Della yelled. Harland pulled the trigger. The shot hit the dust at Della's feet.

A second shot whistled by her head. Della made a run for the truck. She threw open the door and hopped in. Vern had the seat adjusted for his longer legs, and Della didn't have time to fix it. She pulled her weight down onto the clutch and brake, using the steering wheel for leverage. She heard more shots, but she didn't look around to see how close they were. Tears blurred her vision.

She jammed the key into the ignition and made the motor roar. She did some split-second bargaining—she could get the kids out of there tomorrow morning. Or better yet, she decided as she punched the accelerator, she'd come back for them, later that night, with friends for backup. Crystal and her husband would help. The important part was that someone got out.

But as Della sped along their gravel driveway toward the hunk of land connecting their family to the rest of the world, Mylan stepped smack-dab in its center, blocking her way. He waved his arms, yelling for her to stop. She was going too fast for that.

She swerved to avoid hitting him, and the truck went into a skid. During that moment she spun out, she saw the moat come close, its dark water reaching. A white flash of Mylan's pajamas as the truck's wheels slid off the edge of the strip of land. A racing engine. Tires spinning. Her head banging the steering wheel. Warm blood stinging her eyes. Cold water soaking her socks. No sense of up or down, forward or back, home-side or world-side. Her wrist throbbing. The front end of the truck pitching forward from the weight of the engine, the water pressing on the doors, sticking them closed. A shrill cry that came from her own mouth. Thick, hollow silence when she closed her mouth, except for the slurping sound of water filling the truck cab. The fog on the windows from her hot, fast breath. The moat rising to envelope her calves, tickle her thighs. The water lapping up her stomach, telling her something. What was it saying? None of us gets final say. Her head felt heavy. She set it on the steering wheel. The water licked her chin.

She remembered her wedding day, the church all blank, high ceilings—stark as the quarry. As bride and groom left the church through the waiting crowd, a gunshot cut across the happy voices. Vern had plied three of his cousins with a thirty-pack of Natty Light to give him and his bride a three-gun salute. One of the boys had an itchy trigger finger. He shot. A startled flock of grackles rose croaking from an ancient cottonwood. The others hurried to catch up and shot and shot and shot into the sky.

A grackle fell down, hit her ten-year-old flower girl on the shoulder, and stuck there. The girl shook her arms and screamed, but the bird remained. Della rushed over and knocked the bird off with her bridal bouquet. The grackle hit the ground, a ruffled mass of feathers. Blood dripped from the lilies of the valley in her bouquet. "Look at what your idiot cousins did," she said to Vern.

"That bird shouldn't have flown in front of the boys' guns," Vern had told her. "What did it think would happen?"

ALEX LEMON

I Get Collect Calls from Way Up Top

When I think real hard
I can understand every-
Thing—Nuclear peptides.
Hyperlipidemia. Even
The reverse goatee. Once
I thought so intensely
My neighbor doused
Himself in gasoline,
Turned into the Human
Torch in front of McDonald's
Big greasy windows. Ages
Ago, I was voted All-Time
President of the enormous fly-
Whirling mulch pile in
The backyard. The wind
Wolf whistles, whispers
That I am a dictator
But I take off my shirt
So the sky can see my toothy
Scars, the footprint-shaped
Burns that your last Coup
D'état flowered over me.
I never know when you will
Arrive. The truth of it: dark
In the faraway of me I crave
It. When the decaying soil
Is mine, I am a most benevolent
Ruler—the wreck of banana
Peels & coffee grounds is well-
Maintained, massaged by these
Dexterous hands with love,
Precision & grace. There is a man

That someone seems to keep
Shackled in the basement who
Crawls outside, sings lullabies
Into the rot. I could kiss
That fool, but my vigilance
Allows no time for weakness.
Every morning there are hundreds
Of dead birds on the lawn—
Each one to be folded into silk
Panties, thrown like a grenade
Into the public pool across
The street & there, in
The deathy sweetness
That weeps from their beaks,
I smell your surprise—you are
Closing in, always, on my heels,
Right behind me, nearly, sitting
On my shoulder, almost, inside me.

Bugs Need Hugs

Bitch, you crazy,
The dark thickening
Elmgrove whispered.
I cried out, showed
Them that instead
Of thumbs I was
Born with rabbits'
Feet. The hundreds
Of eyes that stared
At me did not blink.
To push back against
The fear, I turned
Myself into a machine
With arms that did
Not stop chopping.
A symphony of slide
Whistles thickened
The brambling dark
With music. I ran one
Hundred miles per
Hour toward the moon-
Light, somersaulting,
Finally, into a shorn
Grass field that looked
Snow-frosted. On
My back, I lay down
In the brightness, trying
To breathe. Like steel
Wool, the glow
Scoured my face
Until my entire body
Roiled. My skin
Tugged as if it was
Tearing away from
The rest of me.
The insects on me

Glinted, churned. Thorax.
Abdomen. Every-
Where, wings. My flesh
Was the surface
Of the ocean. In their
Dice-rattling noise
I heard someone say
That soon, I would
Conquer flight. Above:
A few wayward clouds,
Enormous TVs
Flickering on & off
In each. I tried to
Find my heart by
Using the last tool
I had on me, my mind.
For the first time
I really thought about
Where that bloodbag
Might be hiding out,
But my furry thumbs
Had turned in for
The night. I pushed
Into all of my known
Soft parts with
Everything an arm-
Less man like me
Has. The tiny hope
I had for just a pitter-
Patter or burble
Flushed, flickered,
Then went black.
But around me, night
Spangled joyously.
I traced my stars—
The constellations
I tell no one about—
*Gasoline Can, Man With
Hook Hand* & I felt

Its pumping presence
In me. An oven.
A refinery fire. Impossible
To contain. Endless.
Silent & roaring.

STEFANIE WORTMAN

Crusoe in Utero

When I came to myself I didn't know
this place, whether it was inhabited
or no, or how I traveled here. I saw

at least that the water was abundant
and when I drank, I found it
very refreshing. Exhausted, I lingered

in and out of sleep, sometimes jarred
by nightmares. I quizzed myself,
trying to remember what I knew before.

Who was the king or the viceroy?
Who wrote the Commandments
or the Revelation? Then I cleared

my thoughts and heard only the tide
humming around my island.
I gathered my courage and strength

to travel the shore, surveying my territory,
returning always to where I first knew
despair. The circuit became my daily habit,

a tour of the grounds, which felt
less fearful all the time, more to the scale
of my arms and legs stretching out.

One day, while exploring, I froze
on hearing a voice from nowhere say
Where are you? Where have you been?

How came you here? I fell to my knees
and ducked as if the sound issued from
a demon bird that would momentarily

swoop down to grab me by the throat.
Yet the voice made no request, and why
would a devil speak unless to lure me

into some wickedness? Was it God instead?
Did he land me here? Would he not know
where I had been, better than I did?

I waited, crouched, but the speaker
said nothing more, not then or since,
neither to torment nor give me solace.

I rule this kingdom alone. I take
dominion over everything I touch.
I don't wish myself elsewhere, for I know

nothing of the dangers I could meet
beyond these borders. If I'm designed
to return from exile, fate will offer a hand

to deliver me. I will wait for someone
to speak again, not fill my dreams
with a voice that answers itself.

ADA LIMÓN

The Whale and the Waltz Inside of It

I don't even know how to get to Alaska,
or how to talk about race when the original tongue is gone.

Imagine a woman at the edge, at the border
of the universe waving without an idea
of where to wave, into emptiness, into a bliss?

I moved to New York City once with cash money
I'd saved from being a receptionist for the county and a box
of books I'd never read.

No one tells you how old you'll be one day, or rather,
no one can tell you. Generations are forgotten with their real letters.

Right now, he is trying to explain to me
why whales don't get dizzy, something
about the caves of the inner ear,

but all I see is this spinning, icy black water,
enormous rush, mammalian greatness beneath me,

and how maybe I could swim to Alaska?

I heard about a woman once, maybe she was my mother,
who wanted to move to Alaska, but the bears were trouble.

They gave her a goat to take to the outhouse.

(Not for protection, but for offering.)

It had a little gold bell, the goat,
that rang out in the air like a cannon.

I still worry, even now, about the goat.
Did it know what its job was? Ringing on like that?

I prefer not to make a sound. Will the idea of race go away
        if we all stop talking?

No, we require the goat.

We send people before us, scouts
of air, of water, of fire, of earth,
to tell us how to live.

I want to be the largest animal that ever existed.
The one blue mother—
I'd save the goat, and the bear.

        Did you know giant whales have a spindle cell
        making them capable of attachment
        and of great suffering?

I want to ride around gently and wave
        at the colorful human parade, especially at you,
but in the end I want the watery under.

Evolution, of course.

        (Don't think of the trash the size of Texas.)

Did you know that whales returned to the water?
        It went like this: water, land, water. Like a waltz.

I once had a record of whale sounds,
        I swear I understood.

It didn't matter what worlds they were under,
        what language,
        what depth of water divided,
        the song went on and on.

What I mean is: none of this is chaos.

Immigration, cross the river, the blood of us.
      It goes like this: water, land, water. Like a waltz.

I am in no hurry to stop believing we are supposed
to sway like this, that we too are immense and calling out.

CATHERINE BREESE DAVIS

Railroads

run through

    my life

        like

fire

    cats and

        cars

The father

    of the man

        to whom I

dedicated

    my first book

        was a railroad man

My former

    lover's father

        a Wobbly

who loved

    Raymond Chandler's novels

        was a railroad man

died in an

    accident

        (like

almost

    everyone else)

        My mother's

sister's

    husband

        was a railroad man

The last time

    I saw

        her

(three weeks

        before the sister

                youngest

in a family of nine

        died in an

                accident

of the blood

        cells

                that kept

multiplying

        white

                when she needed

an addition of

        red

                a terrible

mistake

        excessive

                as life

which is

        death)

                I saw him

When I

        was a

                little girl

we lived

        by the railroad tracks

                in South

Bottoms

        Sioux City Iowa

                Whenever

mother

        happened not

                to be home

the hoboes

        we

                my sister and I

fed!
         Two
                  of the best
painters
         I ever knew
                  are railroad men
and whenever I get on a
         train
                  I write
and write
         and
                  write and
you
         Otis
                  whom I keep
track of
         (as best I can)
                  are living
on Railroad Avenue
         that beats
                  all

Teacher

Once
I said something
I've forgotten what

so well

twenty-three heads
together
forgot themselves

bent over their notebooks
set it down
and looked up

expectantly

that was all
but it gave me
pause

I wonder what it was

ADRIAN MATEJKA

The Antique Blacks

—for Sun Ra, Richard Pryor, Guion S. Bluford & the 13
other black astronauts who made it to outer space

In Richard Pryor's origin myth of black
size, the two most magnanimous black men

in the world are peeing off the 30th Street Bridge
into the White River's busted up water. & above,

constellations in the sky's pat afro seem
as indiscriminant as lint in hair & more mundane

lights move lowly on the horizon the way cop
lights always move when black people think

about congregating outside of church. One
brother stares toward Saturn & says, *Man,*

this water is cold. The other looks in the same
direction & says, *Yeah, & it's deep, too.*

•

There's the upward inflection of it—
        the honeyed smile of space
        front & center in our heads—

        Voyager winking
        like a gold incisor
        on its way out
            of this solar system.

Then there's the *because*
& *I-told-you-so* of it—

        slicking its promissory
goatee with a ringed thumb
        & ringed forefinger

right before a bugged-out
        hustle of piano & grin.
Almost & *might be* there again,

        the rounded parts of Saturn
        waiting to go green
                like the cheap metal

under a Jesus piece's already
        sketchy plating.

        The myth of space,
        though.
                It's like *this* wide.

                •

It's like back in Indiana, where my white
mother said, *You are black* because my black
father's jurisdiction includes the skin heliotrope
I'm in. It includes nickel plating four-fingered
rings, fist-picking Cassinis, one-dropping
codes again. Pacers' caps tilting toward Saturn
on their own volition. All things interstellar
are black & white through a telescope—
the Moon, Mars, Voyager—it doesn't matter.
Back in Indiana, we got one channel: TV40,
The Little Rascals & Stymie's meticulous
black & white head as shined up as a Buick
handle when the passenger door shuts. Then
Leave It to Beaver's statutory whiteness cuffed
between corduroy preachers, one after another.
Something happened between those creased
sermons & I was like them that dream, staring
at the bent springs under my brother's bunk,
hand-me-down Millennium Falcon pillowcase

with a circumference of sweat mapping every
one of those faded stars & laser swooshes.
The zig-zag idea of something extraterrestrial.
The sorriest captain of the saddest bottle ship
this side of the White River where there
is always a jumble of something bottoming
the preacher's corked-up jug of canaries & stars.

•

It might squeak like a cork
fitting into an old jug,
          but it's the plutoid
of expectations gerrymandering itself—

enough rough meat left
          to crack the jaw
          of any brother who can't

          play ball. It follows him
across parking lots & into
bagel shops like a rain
          cloud in a cartoon.

The whole thing sounds
like a rocket ship
          cresting a full moon.

          Him & his slick silhouette
while his boys watch him toss up
brick after brick after brick.

Him & his pack of white
friends—a flotilla
of jumpers & pale layups & we're

          all rising up in the gospel
          of headbands & Chuck Taylors

          Tuesday mornings at the Y.

In Indiana, you either play
        ball or deal with abjection

        like a rocket ship
crashed into the moon's eye.

        •

The moon was still out the Tuesday morning I got my first
real curl & Guion S. Bluford became the first black man
into outer space. August 30, 1983. I styled my wet frond
like *Purple Rain* Prince: left side tucked behind my ear, right
side getting activator in the same eye I would have used
to telescope the Challenger as it eclipsed Kennedy Space Center
at midnight in the habit of every brother I have ever met
trying to get away from something without a quotient. Math,
astrophysics—it doesn't matter. It all equals escape. All
those funny words related to space flight, too—*velocity*,
trajectory, *stamina*. In Indiana, any yellow brother with
enough stamina could pretend to be Prince if he widened
his eyes like two afterburners & got a curl. Even in Pike
Townships, where the Pyramids have the exact same velocity
as three cranial lumps rising from skillet hits. Or in Martinsville,
a town so precise with its epithets, billboards, & buckshot,
Guion S. Bluford wouldn't even fly over the place.

        •

Guion S. Bluford is not
Sun Ra any more
        than the *Sounds of Earth*—

        golden in that spinning

        Voyager space probe—
        parlays the real ruckus

we make in our tin
        pan hustle of engine ignition

& *nigger* used as noun & noun
        again in NASA hallways.

Where to begin? Where is
        the smiling headdress
        of planets? Where is

        the smiling astronaut team
portrait, the singular brother
in his Colonel dress—

        ringed in whiteness
like number 1 on these dice?

•

Before 8 - 9 - * - 1 - 4 was catchy enough,
extraterrestrial enough to scare any 10-year-
old babysitting behind a door with a lock
as hollow as a half note, John Williams tried
300 chromatic combinations for the theme
to *Close Encounters of the Third Kind.* Before
the Challenger's third trip to space. Before
Guion S. Bluford confirmed space sounds
the same as Indiana at night only without
the black-masked & scrambling burglars,
black space in nooses, & lightning bugs.

•

Richard Pryor:

I feel it's time black people went to space.
White people have been going to space for years
& spacing out on us, as you might say.

•

        Without the sonic spacing
        of lead in & lead out,

the moon is the same shape

as a record
which is shaped the same
as a vinyl afro
rounding the face in the same

way a crown of stars would
if crowns were stars for anyone

other than Sun Ra—

13 stars clustered around his elbows

& ears & working tape deck. He said:

I'm not part of history. I'm more
a part of the mystery
which is my story

one hand fingering an allegory
of astronaut & ancient prototype
on a piano bench

in Auntie's front room with plastic-
covered furniture, her phonograph
always spins jazz—

right next to a pool hall
ringed by posters

for disco throw downs
& Under-21 battles of the bands—

all of that razzmatazz, all those side
tables & decorative lamps—
well-lit postscripts
to explorers & outer space.

•

Richard Pryor:

We're going to send explorer ships through
other galaxies & no longer will they have
the same type of music—Beethoven, Brahms,
& Tchaikovsky. From now on, we'll have a little
Miles Davis, some Charlie Parker. We going
to have some different kinds of things in there.

•

All lowercase things in here, all spacing

things in here & those words—

    & that vernacular hubbub—

    & that code switch tripping

on curbs in triplicate—

    three fingers on the piano keys,
    three huffed-up hopes on the upswing

of Indianapolis' West Side. Words work

the fast magic like a magician's
fingers fanned out as a W—

    tingling fingers over here, white
    chickens pecking the rain's thin wrist

    over there—
    building a nest egg

on every great crescendo
    of winged g-dropping.

•

This is the g-dropping vernacular
they put in me back then. This is

the polyphone when my head
was an agrarian gang sign pointing

like a percussion mallet to a corn
maze in one of the smaller Indiana

towns. Be cool & try to grin it off.
Be cool & try to lean it off.

I'm grinning to this vernacular
like the bass drum in a patriotic

marching band. Be cool & try to ride
the beat the same way me & Pryor,

Ra, & Bluford did driving across
the 30th Street Bridge, laughing at two

big-headed dudes peeing into the water
& looking at the stars. Right before

the cop hit his lights. *Face the car,*
fingers locked behind your heads.

Right after the patriotic fireworks
started to pop off. *Do I need to call*

the drug dog? Right after the rattling
windows, mosquitoes in my ears as busy

as 4th-of-July traffic cops. Right before
the real thrill of real planets & pretend

planets spun high into the sky, Ra
throwing up the three West Side fingers,

each ringed by the misnomer of me
grinning at an imaginary billy club

down swinging. Because fireworks
light up in the same colors as billy clubs

& rough knuckle ups if you don't
duck on the double. Because the West

Side can be more cold-blooded
& patriotic than any part of Earth

Voyager saw when it took a blue picture
on the way out of the heliosphere.

TRUDY LEWIS

Temple of Pharmacy
1868

SARAH HAD PASSED THE PLACE several times while calling on a patient or buying supplies from the chemist, but in spite of her husband's urgings, she was never able to bring herself to enter the door. The Temple of Pharmacy sat in Lower Manhattan next to Niblo's Theater, and this huge glorified shop, its façade ornamented with marble and its roof topped with a wooden yacht, was almost as dramatic as the neighboring venue for melodrama and musical theater. It was especially glorious when the owner, Dr. Henry T. Helmbold, arrived in his gold-trimmed carriage, the Negro driver deploying the whip to strip first one steed, then the next, of the bunches of violets adorning their ears. James reported that the actors and musicians often came out to watch, tourists and rubes stood staring in the street, and children from the neighborhood gathered in the hope of catching one of the coins the great doctor distributed almost as enthusiastically as he peddled his famous pills and ointments.

Sarah spied the stooped form of her husband, leaning on his ivory-handled cane just outside the door of the shop, and decided to join him, if only to bring him home again. To think that at his age, he would loiter in the street like an errand boy waiting for the master to appear. He had been hankering after Mr. Helmbold for months, and believed, with the single-minded faith of the elderly, that the good doctor represented his only hope for recovery. His talk was all of Helmbold's amazing Extract of Buchu, his racing horses and carriages, his famous customers—among them Boss Tweed, Commodore Vanderbilt, and the Shah of Persia—, his dinners at Delmonico's and his lavish home in Long Branch. Most of all, James spoke of Helmbold's Temple of Pharmacy—the marvelous structure on Broadway, a palace of light and transparency as opposed to the dark unspeakable medical facilities of old. There, medicine was practiced amid perfume and mirrors, and the doctor himself, arrayed in formal dinner attire and the natural wonder of his thick black beard, attended those patients who could afford to be admitted to his inner sanctum for private consultation.

But Sarah, true to her principles, felt little pleasure in the spectacle of a wealthy man displaying his value to the world. She had been tending patients for nearly twenty years without bothering to assume a title or take a medical degree, much less make a public display of her abilities. During her time in the mills at Lowell, she agitated for the ten-hour day, but, left to her own devices, she worked the same twelve-hour shift she had been forced to endure a weaver in the Hamilton. Of course, the labor was lightened by variety and a sense of purpose. Her patients, mostly women and children with respiratory ailments, appealed to her sympathies and she was able, by certain economies, to devote every Monday to serving the poor. Sarah took special pleasure in the homeopathic remedies her husband devised to circumvent the violent bleeding and purging practiced in his youth. She was surprised, in fact, by her delight in the mechanism of the human form. As a young woman, she dreaded human contact, preferring machines for their reliability and words for their precision. But after marrying the widowed Dr. Durno and taking up his profession, Sarah experienced a new comfort with the vagaries of the flesh.

Not that her skill with words had gone to waste. In fact, Sarah still spent much of her time composing text for newspaper ads, circulars, handbills, bottle wrappers, and even calendars and Farmer's Almanacs, applying, in the praise of her husband's nostrums, all the rhetoric she had formerly employed as President of the Labor Society and editor of the *Voice of Industry*. With her aid, the business thrived, becoming so successful that James was able to move Durno's Nostrums from Philadelphia to Albany and then all the way to New York in pursuit of larger markets. The profits from their top-sellers, Durno's Indian Mountain Liniment and Catarrh Sniff, allowed them to rent a warehouse in Manhattan and purchase a modest brick bungalow in Brooklyn.

Nevertheless, James seemed discontented. Ever since the move, he had become querulous, complaining of the heat, the cold, the smells and noises in the street, his son Walt's requests for money to fund unlikely business ventures, and especially the inadequacies of his own body, which, after serving him admirably for upwards of seven decades, began to transform itself, piecemeal, into an engine of waste and shame. Once a proud, stout man with a belly that he carried before him like a ship's prow, he had lost an alarming amount of weight, until his skin hung on his bones as loose as a collapsed sail. Once an enthusiastic lover who introduced Sarah to the pleasures of married love with warmth and good humor, he now expressed little interest in tender contact, but commanded her like a menial, to bare her flesh or mangle his. He had trouble eating even the bland meals prepared for them by their good cook Naomi. He slept very little, and Sarah heard him wandering through the house at night, his halting gait a reprimand to her as she sank down into a deep, muscular sleep. In the morning, his hands shook on the pages of the *Tribune* and he made more and more frequent use of Durno's Catarrh Snuff, his most popular product, until he began to suffer from nosebleeds and palpitations.

True, James was now an old man, ripe for retirement, and wealthy enough to give up the business any time he liked. But his success brought him no happiness, only increasing anxiety. He began to question Sarah's business practices, reading over the account books with a magnifying glass, then moving on, without asking permission, to the personal papers she'd tucked away in odd hatboxes during her brief stint as a milliner. What he found brought him little satisfaction, and he paused with suspicion over the correspondence from the Lowell Ladies Labor Reform Association, the impassioned editorials in the *Voice of Industry* and in particular, those documents relating to Sarah's association with John Cluer, a labor leader and bigamist who had passed through town in the year 1846.

It was at the peak of this investigation that James became fascinated with Henry T. Helmbold, the richest manufacturer of patent medicines in New York. Like the Durnos, Helmbold had begun his business in Philadelphia. There, he manufactured Extract of Buchu from the leaves of a South African plant and promoted it as a cure for a long list of ills: disease of the prostate, irritation of the bladder, gravel, incontinence, diabetes, loss of power, fatuity, and those unmentionable diseases contracted through indiscretions or persistent self-abuse. Sarah remembered the pink pamphlets that littered the city's hotels and public toilets, purporting to be patient's guides to the diseases of the sexual organs. Just before her marriage, she worked as the secretary at the Quaker Rosine's House for Fallen Women, and so was familiar with such sad cases.

But there was no evidence that Buchu had any positive effect on these poor women, just as there was little reason to believe Helmbold could cure James. Walking back to the front of the shop, which took up most of a city block, Sarah watched her husband reach inside his waistcoat to retrieve an ornate silver snuffbox. In the past, he took his snuff directly from his product's commercial package, rich as a velvet pincushion and pink as a healthy lung. But last week, inspired by Helmbold's grand style, he'd purchased the most elaborate snuffbox he could find, a travesty of nude nymphs and rude cupids, with three lurid rubies like drops of blood on its lid.

She waited for James to take his dosage then walked up and took him by the arm. He startled at her touch, his shoulder jerking violently and his handsome blue eyes blinking under thick brows.

"Have you finally come to meet the doctor, then?" he said, recovering himself and tucking the snuffbox into his coat pocket. "After all your shirking?" James was a Scotsman, and even now, after a lifetime in America, his speech was still strewn with thistles and thorns.

"I suppose I am curious to know what you find in the man," she replied.

He gave an extra sniff, expressing contempt, perhaps, or merely testing strength of the snuff in his nostrils, then took her arm and steered her to the door.

Inside, the shop was lined floor to ceiling with mirrors—so many mirrors that Sarah found herself disoriented. The air assaulted her with the smells of licorice, molasses, and alcohol, key ingredients in the Extract of Buchu, and, beyond these medicinal odors, there rose a rich sickening gardenia perfume. The shop itself was crowded with clerks and customers, their noise magnified by the height of the ceiling.

She saw an elderly couple walking toward her, the wasted man dapper as a corpse prepared for a funeral in his black waistcoat, the wizened woman stiff and anxious in a plain gray dress and worsted shawl. Only after a few seconds did she recognize these alien figures as James and herself. How had they become so aged? She moved as swiftly as a hummingbird—travelling, speaking, writing, finding work and executing it as eagerly as if it were some delightful treat to be consumed. And yet time had outrun her, it seemed, as surely as if she had spent her life just sitting still.

She turned away, startled, and nearly crashed into a blue and gold sarcophagus looming above her, its huge headdress nearly touching the ceiling and its smooth surface relieved, at chest level, by a tap.

"This fine fellow is just for display," James said, knocking on the side of the sarcophagus with a familiar gesture. "We will take our refreshment in the parlor."

The room swarmed with clerks in blue uniforms and customers of all ages. They passed back and forth over a black and white marble floor, decorated, at intervals, with a brass inlay of double H's representing Helmbold's initials. Green glass globes hung from the ceiling, also bearing the familiar letters. And everywhere confusion reigned. Customers sat drinking soda at counters. Negro attendants hurried by with mysterious bundles. Men in blue velveteen jackets, who seemed to enjoy some higher status, passed back and forth with newspapers in their hands. Canaries sang in tall gold cages, adding to the cacophony, and little children, freed from any semblance of adult supervision, poked their small fingers between the gilded bars.

Beside her, she felt James' arm quake and his pulse quicken. Oh, what a frustration to be so enfeebled and still so agitated. But without this obsession that had fueled his past few weeks, she wondered whether he would find the energy to continue at all.

They reached the first counter and he pointed to the glass case filled with remedies. A clerk came up to assist them and, noting the dry rash on Sarah's cheeks, recommended the Rose Wash to restore the natural glow of her complexion.

Could he possibly believe that, at her age, she was still vulnerable to vanity? If her cheek was red, this was the inevitable effect of the city's grime. In fact, it was James and not Sarah who appeared red in the face, she thought, as she observed the nose with its broken capillaries and the painful discoloration of the nostrils.

"My dear," he said, with some of the formality of their courtship, squeezing her elbow with a friendly pressure, "would you care to try the rose water? I will be happy to treat you."

Why contribute to Helmbold's bloated empire? Why purchase their competitor's wares? James held out the pretty pink bottle as if offering her a flower. No, she had no need for anything more exotic than soap and lanolin, she said, and handed the bottle back to the attendant with impatience.

"I hoped you would accompany me with an open mind," he said then, his face turning bitter as quinine and assuming the expression he wore when speaking to Sarah about her questionable past. "Mr. Helmbold gives me the solace I cannot find at home. Since you are unable to provide for me, I hope you will express some gratitude toward those who can."

Her heart plummeted in her chest, its dead weight anchoring her to her spot on the marble floor.

James turned away to another counter, continuing to speak, but she could scarcely hear him over the call of the canaries and the murmuring of the customers in the huge, cavernous space.

While she watched, he purchased a handsome bottle of Extract of Buchu, unsealed it, and began drinking without measuring out the dosage. It was shocking to see a man who had been so devoted to precision consuming the extract exactly as a tippler would guzzle spirits in a saloon. He wiped his face with his handkerchief, a new one, she saw, of a rich striped linen. But its only effect was to draw attention to the age spots on his hand and the angry lesion that had appeared just above his wrist, the result, he claimed, of an accident with his shaving knife. Such accidents happened with alarming frequency, and Sarah feared that she would soon have to take charge of the shaving knife herself.

He tucked the bottle into his pocket and once again, took her by the arm. But this time, the gesture contained more force than chivalry, as if he were conducting her to some chamber of punishment. She regretted agreeing to this meeting, and imagined Henry T. Helmbold, as depicted in his advertisements, a man with a charismatic gaze and a black beard so vast that any number of objects might be hidden in its depths. Once again, they passed a mirror, and she ducked her head in the hope of avoiding the deathly image that she had seen before. But this glass was different than the others, a carnival mirror that distorted them as they passed, so that James' form ballooned out, reminding him of his former girth, while hers was diminished beside him.

Midway through the shop, there was a square marked off from the rest of the space by a brass banister, and inside this barrier stood a large public parlor, like a mirage of domesticity in the midst of the marketplace. To either side were glass display cases, filled with bottles and ointments, brushes and hand mirrors, trusses and canes. Here, Negro attendants waited on the customers, the gold buttons on their white coats gleaming, as they handed out newspapers and magazines.

Husband and wife passed into the space, where they sat seated knee to knee, Sarah in a velvet chair and James in a silk rocker. They rarely found themselves in such close proximity and Sarah noted an uncomfortable array of emotions—pity, fear, the memory of desire and the anticipation of some inevitable parting. She had never wanted to marry, or at least not since John Cluer tried to make her party to his bigamy. And yet, she believed she had been happy with her husband. James was a good man, moderate in his habits and generous with his affection, and she was fortunate, after her disillusionment with the labor movement, to find some shared endeavor on which to lavish her energy. But in recent months, her husband's deterioration revealed someone altogether unrecognizable—suspicious, selfish, unkind—who was nothing like the comrade of her middle years but reminded her of the factory owners and overseers back in Lowell. Was this who he had been all along, beneath the façade of fellowship and good will?

To distract herself, she surveyed the other customers, a lady in a veil, no doubt some dance hall actress or courtesan, and a little boy with a wen on his eye who sat sucking his shirt collar. A mother and daughter stood in the vestibule counting out pennies into a handkerchief while across the parlor a young man in a porter's uniform sat with his legs apart wringing his hat in his hands. It did them some good, she believed, to assume responsibility for their own health, to measure out the medicines, to assess the effects, rather than merely submitting themselves to the surgery and the leech. That was why she had agreed to write copy for Durno's. If her prose was somewhat inflated, then it was only in proportion to the deafness of the populace, who had to hear a message shouted and exaggerated before taking it to heart.

Beside her, James was growing restless. He gripped the arms of the rocker and set off at a galloping pace, his thin legs clamped together in determination. "Doctor Helmbold has not arrived yet, they tell me. He is probably visiting his horses or dining with the mayor at Delmonico's. But he promised to meet us at half past two. You will be civil, I hope, and refrain from baiting the good doctor with your cant."

"My dear," she said, forcing herself to lay her hand upon his knee. "There's no need to exert yourself."

"I'm only trying to keep pace with your antics," he said. "You've led me a fine dance for almost twenty years, pretending to be a ministering angel when you are nothing more than a mere dolly mop of the streets."

He paused to remove the snuffbox from his pocket. But his hands shook with a tremor and the open box fell to the floor, spilling snuff onto the patterned rug. Sarah quickly knelt down, feeling the resistance in her stiff knee, and swept what she could into an open magazine. There it was, the familiar moony scent of menthol, the bicarbonate of soda, and the tang of cocaine. The mix appeared slightly different, however, specially mixed for his private consumption. She stood and deposited the residue into the nearest spittoon. Then James grabbed the snuffbox from her and proceeded to take another dab in each nostril, with the furtive look of a woman applying scent while her lover's back was turned.

"Surely you've taken enough for the time being," Sarah said. "You don't even have a cold."

"My life, madam, is one long cold contracted from the chilly climate of our marriage bed." Then he reached inside his waistcoat for the bottle of Buchu, taking another long pull.

The attendant descended on them then with a disapproving look, waiting for a tip that might never come. In his day, James had been known for his generosity, always eager to treat the maid to sweetmeats or present the cook with a fine winter coat. Now she did not wait for him to respond, but handed the attendant a penny along with the stained magazine and exited the parlor. As James descended the step behind her, his cane caught the back of her skirt and he fell with an alarming thud against the ornamental railing. Both Sarah and the attendant rushed to him and when they righted him, she saw there was a knot already forming on his poor bald forehead, like a blue robin's egg nesting above his brow.

"I will be fine, Mrs. Durno, if you can manage to refrain from pushing me into the grave."

The smell of gardenias grew stronger and Sarah saw that their path through the store was blocked by two marble fountains, liquid pouring forth from the mouths of fishes into open oyster shells. This was the source of the rich and cloying perfume that pervaded the shop. On an impulse, she pulled her handkerchief from her pocket and dipped it into one of the fountains, then held it, like a poultice, to the wound on James' forehead. At first, he pushed her hand away. But eventually he gave in and stood there patiently as a horse waiting to be brushed. Something in his flesh was still dear to her, this responsive human core that yielded, like no loom or printing press, to the nuances of touch.

After a few moments, he broke away and led her to the soda counter, where he ordered two glasses, then proceeded to fill them both with extract of Buchu. Sarah wanted to decline, but considering his excitement, she thought better of it, and tasted the doctored soda with curiosity. It was pleasant enough, the molasses and caramel imparting sweetness and the licorice adding some root authenticity to the brew. Thankfully, James downed his glass quickly and did not appear willing to wait for her to do the same. So she left her scarcely tasted soda water on the counter in gratitude, not forgetting to reach into her purse for another penny and leave it there next to her glass.

James was now in a truly altered state. Sarah watched him as he nearly ran into a poor attendant then stopped to stare with outrageous indelicacy at a young woman unbuttoning her bodice to reveal an angry rash.

They passed into the advertising department, where men in blue velveteen jackets scribbled at scroll top desks or sat examining the day's papers. On either side of them, large bins stood filled to the brim with newsprint, like fountains of words constantly collected and reused. Here Sarah paused, struck by the magnitude of the operation. She had written perhaps a bin-full of copy over the course of her career. As a telegraph operator, she transmitted thousands of communications and as the President of the Lowell Female Labor Reform Society, she was required to draft endless notices and speeches, culminating in a vast scroll of signatures she presented to the Massachusetts State Legislature for its review. Yes, she had known her share of words, had tasted and weighed them, spoken and penned them, set them in type and tapped them out over the wires, all in some desperate search of truth. What was it, that motto she had printed? "Truth loses nothing upon investigation." And yet she wondered whether even this bare statement could withstand the encroachment of time. What was it, in fact, that lost nothing upon examination? What was it that did not suffer change? Hadn't she herself become unrecognizable?

She remembered the fateful last interview with Cluer, when, enraged by the charge of bigamy in the paper, he scattered the type of the *Lowell Courier* and then left her to defend him in print the next day. Although she remained the editor of the *Voice* for some months and retained her post as President of the Ladies Labor Reform Society throughout the year, she knew that this had been the true moment of her resignation. She could not continue to work as an apologist for the people. She was compelled to find another profession or feel her soul shrivel inside the shell of virtue she had made.

She moved, as if by fascination, to one of the bins and dipped her hand in its depths, a poor choice, given the local standards of sanitation. There an unpleasant dampness greeted her fingertips. Newsprint, tobacco, mucous? She held on, in spite of her distaste, to retrieve a sheet of newsprint.

James, who was already exiting the department, was forced to turn around and come back to retrieve her. "Please keep your hands out of the rubbage, if you can."

Sarah unfolded the sheet of newsprint to reveal an ad with the iconic yacht— Helmbold's Rose Water, Helmbold's Grape Pills, and of course the major seller, Helmbold's Extract of Buchu. She noted the new recommendations: "used by persons from the ages of eighteen to twenty-five and from thirty-five to fifty-five or in the decline or change of life."

It occurred more frequently than one might expect, the change of life, or rather the changes of living, at fifteen and twenty, thirty-five and fifty-two. Sarah, who had passed through a half dozen occupations and as many cities, was in a unique position to comprehend such radical mutability. She looked down at the paper to review her competitor's claims. Extract of Buchu came highly recommended to treat discoloration of the kidneys, retention of the urine, mucous or milky discharges, indisposition to exertion, loss of power, loss of memory, difficulty of breathing, weak nerves, trembling, horror of disease, wakefulness, dimness of vision, pain in the back, hot hands, flushing of the face, and universal lassitude.

Who, she wondered, had been lucky enough to escape all of these ailments? Who could remain immune to such a claim? Could religion compete with it? Could justice hold up to it? Could even science dispute its appeal? She no longer wondered at James' attraction to the man or his establishment, but only wished that she could find some way to give her husband what he so obviously craved.

"Hurry along then, Madame Editress."

They passed yet another mirror, in which Sarah spied a flash of her former self, the trim woman of middle years, her face unlined, her hair as brown as earth. This was the woman who, famed throughout the mills for her virtue, had still fallen in love with a duplicitous man. If she could make that mistake at the height of her powers, how could she blame James for falling prey to a charlatan in the decline of age?

In the waiting room, a well-dressed couple sat holding hands on a velvet chaise. James settled himself on a gilded chair and began fumbling with his snuffbox, like a child worrying the lock of a music box. The canaries sang out in a sharper tone as the shop filled up with the crowd from the theater and Sarah thought of the golden nightingale in the story, the mechanical bird that sang the emperor to sleep but could do nothing to save him from death. She leaned over James and released the latch of the snuffbox noticing the sigh of the springs.

At the very back of the shop sat Helmbold's examination room, a glass-enclosed parlor with the words "Sanctum Sanctorum" printed in gilt lettering over the door. Inside, she could make out a large desk and a tall dark column. Tensing her calves, she swung her short legs over the floor in impatience. She hated to cease her labor in the middle of the day. She did not have the time to waste, or the energy to sit still. Even if she had an afternoon clear of appointments, she could still be writing out a new advertisement, reading over her notes, or straightening her rooms. Once she finally found a comfortable position leaning on her side and cradling her arthritic elbow, she fell into a sleep as deep and comforting as if she were lying in her own bed at home. In her dream, she was back in Lowell again, sitting at the window of Climena's dress shop sewing a straight seam into a plain blue woolen dress. She felt a great pride in what she had accomplished. The sun was just setting and a crowd of operatives passed by in the street, walking toward the boarding houses and their evening meals, their twelve hours of labor completed at last. Then Cluer appeared at her side naked, as he never had in life, and she saw that she was in danger of ruining all she had worked to achieve.

Just as she touched him, she awoke with a powerful sense of relief, and lifting the watch from the ribbon around her neck, she saw that it was now half past three and the doctor had not yet appeared. Beside her, James fidgeted with his empty snuffbox, and jiggled his knee against hers. The knot on his forehead had grown larger, in less than an hour's time, and the bare area between his nose and lips, where he had once worn a mustache, was now entirely pink with irritation. Sarah set her hand on his knee and he jumped and gave a yelp, high and broken as a winded horse. When had his voice changed so dramatically, from the rich baritone she had loved to this whine as pitiful as a child's?

Then the door of the office opened and the doctor himself emerged, steering forth the couple she had seen in the waiting room earlier. They were of a ripe middle age, the man balding and the woman plush with extravagant flesh. The doctor himself looked as if he had been dancing a quadrille. He wore an evening jacket with silk lapels and a vest embossed with golden fleur-de-lys. His full black beard was so long that it nearly obscured his cravat, and his face flushed red with self-regard. Meanwhile, his assistant, dressed as a footman, stood and lifted Sarah by the hand. The man's gloves were of such delicate kind that they aroused her nerve tips, reminding her of the sensuality of her dream.

James collected himself and stood without assistance. His face assumed some of its old intelligence, then clouded over with glassy veneration. Horrible, horrible, that the husband she had married in a spirit of equality now found himself in thrall to a lesser, if more extravagant, man. She looked away, toward the front of the shop, to avoid having to witness the sight. But she only encountered her own image again, in yet another cursed mirror. This time, she saw a woman with flushed cheeks, younger, perhaps than she had appeared earlier in the day, yet also more agitated.

"My good fellow," Helmbold said, clasping her husband's hand and holding it in his own, if he considered the poor man too weak to withstand a handshake. "I am pleased to find you in such delightful company." Could the doctor really be of such small stature? Scarcely taller than herself, he nevertheless conveyed an aura of immense size and strength.

Inside the office, Sarah smelled extract of Buchu, emanating from Helmbold's person along with the medicinal odor of the eucalyptus plants that lined the walls. And in the center of the room stood a huge carving of Helmbold himself, executed in exotic dark wood. This totem stood over eight feet high, guarding the office like a pagan god.

"Mrs. Durno, your husband has been consulting me on a matter of some delicacy." His voice was too big for the room, loud and metallic as the clanging of machines on the factory floor.

"There is no need to employ euphemisms, Doctor. I am a woman of plain speech and considerable experience."

"That is my fear. You have noticed your husband's complaints?"

She looked at James and saw that he did appear improved, simply by absorbing the presence of his idol. Could it be that the doctor was doing him some good after all?

"Mr. Durno suffers from a number of ills," she replied. "Most of them due to his age."

"Age is not a death sentence, Madam. In this modern era, a man can live well into his ninth decade in reasonable health and vigor, given proper medical care and a happy home. In your husband's case, however, I believe there is another cause for his infirmity."

"Dr. Helmbold says I am infected with syphilis," James announced, with as much satisfaction as if he were informing her of a victory over a rival or the unexpected recovery of a patient in his care.

Sarah winced, thinking of his frustrations, and how he had, for some months, staged forced expressions of a desire he did not feel. "And how did you arrive at such a condition?"

"The good doctor believes I contracted the disease from you."

Sarah absorbed the blow in the depth of her entrails, but tried to keep a clear head. She wondered how much James had paid Helmbold to produce such a diagnosis. "And you reached this conclusion through my husband's story alone? I hardly regard that as scientific method."

"I stand willing and able to conduct a medical examination. That is, with your permission, of course." And here he bowed, as if merely inviting a lady to join him in a dance. His red face was flushed with his own product and his hand shook as he pointed, with some force, toward a Chinese screen at the corner of the office.

So this was the purpose of the visit. That she might be examined. That her very body might be searched for the truth of her husband's decline. She shuddered and leaned forward in her chair.

"Did you or did you not meet Mr. Durno when employed at a house for fallen women?" the doctor asked.

"I was a secretary in the establishment, not a resident."

"And did you not, before that time, have relations of an intimate nature with a bigamist, one John Cluer?"

"He was my associate in the Ten-Hour Movement," Sarah said. "And the accusations against him were never proven."

"Nevertheless, my dear, you must admit you led quite a life before I took you in." James appeared confident now, as he had at the height of their courtship, when he escorted her around Philadelphia showing her the places where Durno's Nostrums were advertised and sold.

"Took me in?" she said, repeating the phrase until she could fashion some rational response.

Helmbold grasped onto his lapels and sat on his desk, so that his striped socks showed to advantage. Beside him, the statue gleamed, impervious to the permutations of age or chemical intervention. He launched into a long disquisition about the natives of South America and their admirable open attitude toward relations between the sexes. He understood that a lady of Mrs. Durno's age and station must labor under a certain degree of modesty. He knew that submitting to an examination would cause her embarrassment. But her husband's cure required that she should sacrifice modesty to reason and prudery to scientific investigation.

Sarah looked at James and tried to assess whether he had brought her here in a spirit of revenge or mere confusion. Was it so painful to lose his powers that he felt compelled to humiliate her as well? Anger and pity mixed in an unpalatable nostrum, and she felt her throat close.

"In any case, I'm certain you will do whatever is necessary to relieve your husband of his affliction," the doctor said, nodding, with mock discretion, in the direction of the cherry blossom screen.

Sarah stood then, and walked toward the corner of the room with deliberation. Was this her final judgment, to be stripped of her dignity and examined like a common prostitute?

Her head pulsed with all the rhythms she had known—the mill wheel, speeding up to force more labor out of its operatives, the tapping of the telegraph, the tender alternation of pressure and release as she palpated a patient's chest. What was she, after all, but a collection of these rhythms, not the inert physical fact of her body, but the unshackling of life's possibilities, one by one, until there was nothing left but sheer unimpeded flow?

She lifted the screen, no heavier, really, than the frame on a loom, and carried it to the doctor's side. She considered striking him with it or asking him to remove his own clothes. Then, seeing the malevolent gleam of the statue, she merely dashed the item at the idol's feet, piercing the screen's delicate tissue.

"You may dazzle all of New York, Mr. Helmbold. You may dine with the mayor and sup with the president. But I believe you are in no position to examine me."

Helmbold slid off his desk and stood in amazement, while James made a feeble attempt to intercept her at the door.

But Sarah pushed past him and rushed through the shop, the tears blurring her vision, so that she saw, as she passed each mirror, strange reflections of the many lives she had known. The child Sarah Bagley climbing up the Granite Mountains. Sarah the weaver, fastest operative on the floor. Sarah the editor, Sarah the doctor. The good wife, the trusty labor leader, the writer of advertisements, and the bigamist's whore. So many women, and which one should be judged? She herself could not make an assessment, but only watched the images as they spun out with the speed of her passing and just as quickly disappeared into the shop's crowded floor.

After her interview with the doctor, she preferred to travel home alone. But she feared for her husband's safety, compromised as he was. To her surprise, however, James caught up with her at the front counter, looking sheepish and fingering the fringe of her shawl. How had be managed to move so quickly, with his physical limitations? How had he escaped Helmbold's spell? She was so relieved that she bought an extra bottle of Buchu on the way out the door and vowed to take his medicine with him, if he still believed it would do him any good.

ROBERT LONG FOREMAN

Why I Write Nonfiction

I DON'T DO IT FOR the money. In the ten years I've spent writing nonfiction, I have made just over two thousand dollars from it. I'll admit it is more than I thought I would ever make from writing, when I was twenty-four and hadn't written anything yet.

I had considered writing something at twenty-four, but had not yet concluded it was really for me. I am still not sure it is, which is part of why I've asked myself why I do it.

The reason I write—nonfiction or otherwise—is not that I cannot resist the challenge posed by writing. There is nothing I find easier to resist than a challenge.

Nor is it that I have been so successful so far that there's no reason to turn back. My next creation is not hotly anticipated by anyone, nor is it anticipated coolly, or lukewarmly. If anything, there are people out there dreading my next work of nonfiction. One of them is my father. He objects to nearly everything I write, and I haven't even written about him yet.

I really don't know why I write nonfiction.

I could stop there, and make this the briefest-ever essay of the Why I Write variety, but instead I'll be ambitious and pursue the question despite the blank I draw when I try to answer it.

•

WHEN I CHOSE TO CALL this essay "Why I Write Nonfiction," I knew that an easy answer was not within reach, which means it is probably worth writing about.

It deserves some qualification, for in the last three years I've written only 800 words of creative nonfiction. The rest of my output has been fiction: thirteen short stories, a novella, and a novel. Some of those things have been published. Some have not.

I never thought I would write fiction, not for the first six years I spent writing, nor for the twenty-four years that preceded them. And it strikes me now that as hard as it is for me to determine why I write nonfiction, it is easy to say why I write fiction.

I know why I started, anyway.

It began like the opening scene of a horror movie.

My wife and I went for a week to a cabin on the shore of Lake Michigan, where we were supposed to finish working on our books. She was revising her first book of poems. I was there to work on a memoir about inheritance. It told the story of my aunt Posy, who died and left me and my five siblings an oversized house that smelled like cigarettes, plus a great many other things that smelled like cigarettes.

By the time we made the trip to the cabin by the lake, I had finished the memoir—sooner than expected—and didn't want to look at it anymore. So Stefanie worked on her book while I sat on the porch drinking coffee and watching the horses who lived at the stable next door. It was cold, so I wore a jacket. I sat in my jacket and stared at the horses for so long that had they not been horses they would have called the police.

But horses don't have police. And I didn't write a thing until our last day there, at which point I started to write my first short story.

I had chosen to take a break from nonfiction, because writing the inheritance book had been a draining ordeal. Writing any book is a draining ordeal. George Orwell says so himself, in the original "Why I Write." "Writing a book," he says, "is a horrible, exhausting struggle, like a long bout of some painful illness. One would never undertake such a thing if one were not driven on by some demon whom one can neither resist nor understand."

So there was that, plus, I had just spent two years writing about a loved one who had died suddenly, a victim of her addictions. I had read the many diaries she'd kept, and been a witness to fifty-nine years of suffering I could not alleviate, for its sufferer had committed already what she called "passive suicide." I had squeezed my heart dry, writing about this stuff.

Enough, I told myself. *Write fiction*. I wrote a story about a man who finds a human brain in the woods and brings it home.

This doesn't explain why I've continued to write fiction since that first resigned turn to the genre. But it does lead me back to why I write nonfiction.

Or, rather, why I used to write nonfiction and will do it again, inevitably. Or why I wrote that memoir in particular, despite how depleting I knew it would be—so much so that I am willing to say today, unironically, that it "squeezed my heart dry."

I could have made that memoir a novel. I could have rendered my aunt a fictional character, sidestepped her diaries—or just skimmed them—made her more overtly interesting, made myself a different person, and come up with a different book entirely, one I could have kept at a safer distance as I wrote it and that might have stood a chance of getting published.

But the book had to be nonfiction, I thought, because the very reason that one fraction of Posy's estate had ever come my way, setting the writing of the book in motion, was that my name had appeared in writing, on her will. "Robert Long Foreman," it had said, on a list of beneficiaries that included the names of my brothers, sister and cousin.

It was a written document that made my inheritance possible, that implicated me in Posy's death by giving to me some of what she'd had. And so, I thought, if I was to write Posy's name somewhere, it should be in a context where it would be similarly freighted with the weight of the world. The memoir I wrote was to be written and read with a constant awareness that Posy had lived and died in the universe that we—the reader and I—shared with her.

The book was to be as invested in the real world as the will was, even if it wasn't such a great means for exerting my will on the world, especially since no one read it.

•

I TEACH CREATIVE NONFICTION, AND had a student in one of my workshops who told me and his classmates, several times, that when he got a submission from another student he took a razorblade and slashed from the manuscript the name of the person who wrote it. He held one manuscript up for us to see. Sure enough, where a name should have been on the first page was a blank, transparent box.

I found it worrisome, and not only because this man apparently kept razorblades in the same place where he did his homework.

You can cut the author's name off a short story without necessarily affecting how you read the story. The same goes for a poem; certainly "You and I Are Disappearing" is the poem it is with or without its author's name hanging over it.

It might even help, in a fiction or poetry workshop, to disregard the name of the author of the work that's in front of you, in order to ensure that your reading of it isn't dogged by what you know of that person, or what you think of her. This is especially helpful when you're a man who holds things up while talking about sharp objects.

But while a good essay or memoir will be a good essay or memoir no matter what, it is dangerous to take a razorblade and slice an author's name away from one, and not only because you might cut your fingers.

This other danger was illustrated for our workshop one afternoon when we discussed the work of one of the other students, a young woman who had written about having sex with her boyfriend. She portrayed herself as the dominant party, the one who tears the other person's clothes off and is in control of the situation. The language she used reflected this. It was blunt. When referring to a certain part of his body, she used the word "shaft," which is a straightforward, maybe unflinching way to refer to a penis—not that they are things that ought ordinarily to be flinched at necessarily, but certainly "shaft" is a more brazen word than "penis" is.

The razorblade man, who never held back in workshops, of course, made a bold statement. He said that because of some of the language used in the piece—I think he was referring to the word "shaft"—he could not accept that its narrator was a woman. He said that some of the words used in the piece were totally male (I am paraphrasing), and that to use some of the words she used (I really do think he meant the word "shaft") was, essentially, to write as a man. "I picture this writer," he said (and here I am not paraphrasing), "as a man—a gay man."

This kind of thing is well worth saying in a fiction workshop, where the narrator of a first-person story is almost never understood to be the author—where you can change the gender of the narrator at will, if it suits you and it's good for the story. But the narrator of an essay or memoir is nearly always understood to be the author, or a representation of her, and she is sitting in the room with you when you discuss her work.

When the razor student said that he felt his classmate's work had to be the work of a man, despite all contrary evidence, this was taken to mean that certain parts of our language, like the word "shaft," were not available to her. If she used them, she was writing more like a man than a woman.

This was how the rest of the workshop took it, anyway, and you can't say that sort of thing in a room filled with liberal arts students and expect not to have to answer for it. Someone told him what he'd said was "sexist" and from there it got ugly.

•

AMONG THE THINGS I DID not tell the students in that nonfiction workshop is that I am, by my own measure, a failure at writing nonfiction.

It is not something I say lightly, which is why I made it a one-sentence paragraph.

I have published essays in literary magazines, and I teach nonfiction workshops. And I have continued publishing since I wrote the inheritance book. But it seems as though I have gone as far as I can in the genre. I can keep writing my little essays and short-form autobiography, and maybe make another two—who knows, even three—thousand dollars in the next eight years. But that is likely to be it. My train has reached the station, and I think there are no more stations after this one.

I make admitting this sort of thing look easy, but it isn't; it has taken years of disappointment and idle griping for me to reach the point where I can say that my nonfiction career may well have run its course.

I think I should have mentioned this to my last batch of students, that I'm a non-fiction failure. I think it is how I ought to have introduced myself—if only because a fair number of my nonfiction students tend to admit defeat on the first day.

They enter the workshop on a whim, as an afterthought, usually because they have written poetry for the last two years and have been overwhelmed by it. They have had it with whatever it is that goes on in poetry workshops—the critiques, probably, and the self-doubt that should not but can come from sustaining them. They have thrown up their hands and they are done with poems. Some even seem to consider themselves failures at poetry, or at fiction, which is funny—to me, not to them—because most of them are twenty or twenty-one and will snap out of it.

But as temporary failures in one genre they are in exactly the right place to start writing creative nonfiction.

I think there is no better time to write nonfiction, and write about it, than after having given up. Some of the greatest essay personae are the deflated ones, the men and women who have turned away from something and taken up writing the genre in resignation—like Montaigne, who retired from public life before he began writing his *Essais*; E. B. White, who left New York City for a farm in Maine before writing his best essays; and Thoreau, who retreated from the world as lived by others in favor, temporarily, of Walden Pond.

It isn't quite the same thing, but many great book-length works of creative nonfiction are, essentially, assessments of what went wrong—like James Baldwin's *The Fire Next Time*, *A Small Place* by Jamaica Kincaid, James Agee and Walker Evans's *Let Us Now Praise Famous Men*, Joan Didion's *Salvador*, plus most of everything else Joan Didion wrote, and other books, too. Nonfiction writers are often at their best when we find them sifting through wreckage of one sort or another.

So there are worse conditions for me to be in as I try to determine why I write nonfiction. The best place for me to be, at least rhetorically, is at the end, or the simulated end, the point where I have admitted defeat, at least for the time being.

And I have earned my claim to failure. I have failed to captivate any editor whose desk has been crossed by one or the other of my book manuscripts (there was another one before the inheritance book, and it, like certain of my relatives, is dead). I should not have probably written those books, and years after spending years at a time writing them I can finally admit that.

This is not a tragedy. I am fortunate to have the problems I have, with food to eat and a healthy daughter who as she grows so does her vocabulary and appreciation for Muppets. But it returns me to the question again of why I continue to write, suspecting, as I do, that I've gotten as far with writing nonfiction—maybe even writing, period—as I can go.

•

My admission of failure does not mean that I'll never again write nonfiction. Even if I declared that from now I would only publish fiction, I know that I could not abandon nonfiction forever. It is the one genre I know I will have to write in, sooner or later, whether I want to or not.

On the day my daughter, Moriah, was born, I remember thinking to myself that now that she was there and healthy I was probably going to have to give a wedding speech at some point in the next thirty-five years or so. And because I am a work horse I started writing it in my head, right there as I was holding her. I thought it should start, "On the day Moriah was born, I thought one thing: Great, I'm going to have to give a wedding speech eventually." And I knew it would be a bad speech, because I would be one of those dads who tries to be funny in the speech he gives at his daughter's wedding and elicits polite laughter. There are worse things than that, but I went to a wedding once where a dad gave a speech that wasn't funny, it was deadly serious, and even I cried, because it was beautiful. So not even a day into my daughter's life she was reminding me what an inadequate writer I am, how I'll always default to cheap humor when what's needed most is grave lucidity.

I don't know if a wedding speech is creative nonfiction. I am inclined to say that it is. It all depends on how you define creative nonfiction, how wide you perceive its generic net to be. When I was younger, I liked to think any crafted narrative that was meant to be taken as truthful or accurate was an example of creative nonfiction. If you accept that, then it appears everywhere, in speeches, in messages written on greeting cards. It is there whenever someone wants to communicate something to another person, or other people, and create the effect of closing the distance between author and reader. That's not to say that greeting card messages are micro-memoirs, or essays; I would not place my wedding speech-in-progress in company with Amiri Baraka's *Blues People*.

But I know that when I was still a young man, and my flower had not yet faded, this ubiquity of creative nonfiction, as I saw it, was one thing that made the genre more appealing than any other. It seemed preeminently visible to me—and it still seems to me that nonfiction prose has, since maybe the nineteenth century, overtaken poetry as the reigning genre of occasional writing.

Most people are intimidated by poetry and feel certain they couldn't possibly write it. Even students in creative writing classes are reluctant to read or talk about poetry. Fiction can be daunting, though not quite like poetry.

But everyone is convinced he can write nonfiction. No one says that writing a memoir must be hard. A lot of people say that it's so easy to write a memoir there is no reason to write them, that no one should even read them. I've been at parties with people like this, and when they find out I've written a memoir it can get ugly.

•

IN THE SPRING OF 2012, in Missouri, I asked the students enrolled in my nonfiction workshop to write essays titled "Why I Write," in the tradition of George Orwell and Joan Didion, whose essays we read.

I had set them up for failure. I hadn't meant to. It is rare for a writer to know why she writes—or at least it's hard to find one who is willing to name her reasons forthrightly. A study in writerly gracefulness, Didion addresses the question throughout her essay without tripping into its crosshairs; I had hoped the students would likewise sidestep the assignment and use it as a prompt for thinking on paper about writing without getting hung up on what it asked them.

It was a poor assignment. I should have known better.

In their Why I Write essays, several of the students said they wrote in order to make people laugh. But they weren't very funny, and they hadn't been all semester. I don't doubt that among their friends they were accomplished humorists, but their attempts at comedy in writing fell flat. They didn't know a certain thing that I know, which was that to be funny in person and to be funny on paper are different things that rarely coincide in one person. I said this several ways throughout my semester with them, none of which were blunt enough to make an impression.

About five students said they wrote simply because they couldn't live without writing. They had to write, or else they would lose their minds.

It is a fine answer, one I've given to the same question the few times I've been asked it directly. But it doesn't address what the question implies, which is: why do you not only write, but spend a great deal of time producing your work, then editing and seeking an audience for it? People don't do those things because they'd lose their minds if they didn't, and it's not unlikely that you will lose your mind if you try it long enough without success, like I might soon.

There were other students in the workshop who gave smart, thoughtful responses, but I have forgotten what they were.

And incidentally, like some of my students in Missouri, my aunt Posy was someone who wrote because she would go crazy if she didn't. Unlike my Missouri students, she did stop writing and went crazy, though it's not clear which one caused the other, and now that I've written it down I realize it's not fair to say she went "crazy." She died, is what happened, but I think she might have been crazy when she died. I don't know. I was hundreds of miles away.

Some of the things she wrote in order to prevent herself from going crazy were my favorite parts of the book I wrote, and it broke my heart to remove them from the manuscript before it started getting sent to editors. They came from the many diaries she kept, starting when she was a teenager. I couldn't find a way to make them fit.

In 1970, she wrote, in reference to I don't know who, "The 7 of us were going to get dematerialized and god god what will we do? David and I must find a place to go." In 1986, she wrote, "You cannot face Death when Death is wearing the mask of your face without that event having a major impact on your life . . . if you live. And I have lived."

This is the work of someone who knew why she wrote. She did it for self-preservation, though in the end writing was not enough to save her.

•

WHILE I WAS AWAY FOR a summer, once, a woman who subleased my apartment in Athens, Ohio, left her dirty laundry behind when she left. There it was to greet me, on the floor of my closet, when I returned.

I faced a dilemma in the dirty laundry. What was I to do with it? I refused to throw it away. Its owner had left the country without making any plans I knew of to return. Her underwear was my responsibility. So I wrote about it, in an essay in which I puzzled over my relationship to these things of hers that were now mine, for which I had no use.

There is a problem with that essay that makes itself plain every time I lay eyes on it, which I had to do recently when, after eight years of revision and submission and more than sixty rejections from literary magazines, it was accepted for publication. Since I wrote it I have changed and grown—not physically, but in my head and heart. I have matured. My face hasn't changed much, and my name is the same, but I have become someone other than the young man who found a woman's clothes in his closet and saw in them a dilemma.

I know, today, exactly what I would do if I found a strange woman's underthings in my house. I would throw them away before my wife came home. But all those years ago, when I found the laundry in my Ohio apartment, I didn't have a wife, and throwing the subletter's bras and stuff away did not seem like an option, somehow.

It is one small indication of something that seems to me very significant.

There is a great distance between me and the person represented in that essay, who is also me; between the one who is writing "Why I Write Nonfiction" in a bakery in Providence, Rhode Island, and the one represented by the pronoun "I" in that other essay, which I started writing nine years ago in Athens, Ohio.

The "I" of the laundry essay showed up in print this year, but it is an old "I," one that isn't really me anymore. That first-person pronoun, which recurs 117 times throughout the essay, is there to tell the world that I have certain anxieties, laundry-related, that I don't really, currently have. It makes real and new an old, long-gone predicament. Every time someone reads it, which I'll admit not many have probably done, I tell that person private thoughts I haven't thought in nearly a decade.

I made every effort to be honest and forthright when I wrote the essay, and to wrestle with a problem that felt real to me. But my honesty and forthrightness have been undermined since 2005, when I solved the problem of the subletter's clothing by donating them to the Salvation Army.

Despite this, the laundry-worried "I" wants to cling to me, the way the "I" of no short story ever would.

And who knows when the "I" I've been using in this essay will make its way into print, will appear somewhere with a date attached, a way of marking that "I" in time. Who knows if I will or will not identify then with the things I am writing now.

It doesn't even take as long as that, for the "I" of an essay like this one to divorce itself from the person it refers to. Earlier in this essay, I mentioned that prior to writing this I had not written nonfiction in several years. But writing this has meant putting down more than 4,000 words of nonfiction. I declared myself a nonfiction failure, but to be honest I feel slightly less like one of those than I did when I started this essay eighteen months ago.

Merely addressing the distance between me and creative nonfiction has necessitated the closing of that distance.

I don't know how to resolve this problem. I don't know that it is a problem. And I think I might spend the rest of my writing life determining why I write and why I write nonfiction. I think I could write indefinitely, in pursuit of a straight answer, and die, or quit, before I came up with one.

There are grad students I have met at conferences who I am glad are not here. They would insist that this thing I have been remarking on—the disconnect between the "I" of my old essay and my present self—is further evidence of the impossibility of nonfiction; that all writing is fiction, no matter what; that there is no difference between fiction and nonfiction, because rendering the so-called real world in writing necessarily distorts it and turns it into fiction.

I have prepared a defense against this argument, for the next time it comes up again. I will, when it does, faint suddenly.

If I do that I won't have to try to account for why we have a thing we call nonfiction that I didn't invent. I won't have to tell the grad student, or whoever it is, that as far as I am concerned it is not up to me to defend this genre; that it's his job to explain why, if all writing really is fiction, there is still a thing we call nonfiction that so many people seem to believe in.

By the time I wake up the subject will have turned to the reason why I just fainted, which I'll lie about.

TROY JOLLIMORE

The Black-Capped Chickadees
of Martha's Vineyard

1

What are birds, what can they be if not
objectified thoughts? That scarlet tanager
an idea about beauty, that American redstart
the memory of a hotel on the Oregon
coast, where you stayed for three days, while the things
you thought you'd understood fell to pieces around you . . .

2

The black-capped chickadee is native to most
of North America, and everywhere its song
is the same. Everywhere, that is, except
on Martha's Vineyard. The black-capped chickadees
of Martha's Vineyard sing the standard
black-capped chickadee song: *hey sweetie,*
hey sweetie—but they sing, as well, a pair
of variations: *sweetie hey, sweetie hey,*
and *soweetie-sweetie, soweetie-sweetie.*
Recordings exist and can be consulted.
As for explanations, the human researchers
who study these things assure us
that they are forthcoming.

3

First you learn to cause pain, then you must learn
to live with having caused pain. There are places
where the mind is permitted to wander unleashed,

and you learn, over time, where the gates are, who keeps them,
under what conditions you will be allowed
to pass unobstructed. You learn the dialects
of rivers, which gestures in which territories
are taken as insults. Knowledge is stored
in the brain in folds of tissue, as is
the memory of your first lover's face,
the melody line of "Someone to Watch
Over Me," and your opinion as to which
of the dozen or so versions of that song
you have heard is the sweetest, the most beautiful,
the most haunting. Though of course your opinion
is subject to change, to a minor rearrangement
of the tissues, one that might be caused
by a shower of petals, an oddly placed word
in an argument with a friend, or happening
to hear that song on the radio
while driving while cruising the stations or in
a bright, slightly musty Parisian café
that you ducked into only to get away from
the spatter of rain that came out of the sky
with no warning, from nowhere at all. *Sweetie, hey.*

4

The nightingale, Pliny writes, is "the only
bird the notes of which are modulated
according to the strict principles
of musical science." Each one, he goes on
to tell us, has its own repertoire
of songs, deployed in the musical battles
they conduct with one another. "The vanquished one
frequently perishes in the contest,
and would rather yield its life than its song."

The part of me that would like to believe this
has taken to walking the creekside trails
late in the evening, when the darkening
sky turns them all shades of blue, hoping

to meet, by chance, if chance is the word,
the twilit part of you that would like
to believe this, which is also the part,
if I'm not mistaken, that wishes to love something,
anything, with the degree of passion
the dying nightingale feels for its song,
the part of you that stood in the open
doorway in a long white dress and said
You talk a good game, but let's not forget,
you're a poet. You'd rather sing about it
than live through it.

5

What I know is this: when you are done learning
how to cause pain, which you never are,
you learn how not to, which you never do.

And what I know is this: early this morning,
in the branches of my neighbor's oleander,
I saw a spot of flame, a spark-red
northern cardinal, out of place
and out of season. And surely, my love,
that has to count for something.

HAILEY LEITHAUSER

Prayer

I do not care for beautiful women;
I do not care.

Calumnious women, even they
can bore by mid-day, and rich

women have nothing
to offer
but the fashions of passionless art.

Send me, Kuan Yin, instead,
a woman of large foot
with a pannier of mussels,
and a stained chef's coat.

Send me, Saint Catherine,
a woman who comprehends
wine,
who will fill my glass, then bandy
me in bed
like a cork on a black sea wave.

KENDRA DeCOLO

The Retired Contortionist Inside You

Sprawled atop the bed
of a truck where high school boys

suck tequila from your neck,
your body anonymous

as a lesser comet,
nipples smeared like emergency

flares, it takes three men
to fasten the jacket,

hold you while a needle
spits serum

into your blood
but I remember how we slept

feather boa and margarine-
hearted, evicted

from every karaoke bar
and dormitory, absinthe-

lit and rolling under bad
sound systems, the rash

of synthetic underwear
and static staining our skin.

I didn't know what was
waiting when I cupped

my ear to your ribs,
a constellation of sores

and glands rasping between us,
how I would be the one

you'd call, years later, your voice
dry and reaching through

the hospital payphone
asking for help, a retired

contortionist unfolding
inside you, waiting

to spill back into the world
like gasoline.

JENNIFER GROTZ

Hangover in Paris

Sunlight hurts. My hair hurts.
My skin crawls as I come to realize where I am,

what I'm hearing. The *Salon de Tatouage*
next door, on Rue de la Roquette.
I'm awake enough to realize it, not enough to enjoy

how that sound (a bug zapper?, a muffled drill)
filters and grows metaphorical

while an artist and his client smoking in the courtyard
energetically debate
what the client will get inked into his arm.

I'm getting moody about permanence, not about
the weird abundance of the temporary, little mushrooms

that come up out of nowhere and disappear in a powdery puff
when stepped on accidentally. I think of *Nausea,*
when Sartre's character grows so disgusted with existence

he writes in his journal: "Did nothing. Existed."
How maybe the former deprivation generates the latter.

How *in terms of the mythic, the historical,*
and of course the aesthetic, the two men have decided
on a spider. That ominously silent, eavesdropping creature.

RANDALL MANN

Secondment

In Basel, gnats appeared in the corners
of my room in the Messeplatz, no wish. I fished
hair and my own gloop from the shower—
lingering—spent evenings fingering

remotes in hopes of BBC 1 through 4, soft-core
cooking shows. I know. Forty's a bit late
for the grand tour. I caught a lot of the Eurovision.
At week two, an NYU student flew in, a little shy

of 21. I thought you said you were,
I thought. (My regret like a coat of spit.)
I thought about getting an animal. About golf.
I worked behind a big oak desk, someone's third-

hand idea of clout. The things I heard.
Freedom was a breezy lie, as was loneliness.
On the sly, I logged on to Planet
Romeo, for flesh: a torso wrote, *I want to dress*

you up like Norway, and invade. Let's forget it.
I went to Istanbul to see Mr. NYU, there
on a summer grant. I did it, but I can't.
In Kuzguncuk, a matted cat crawled out of filth

just to nuzzle me, my face. And I let it.

HEATHER ALTFELD

Fabergé in Lausanne

In the world inside the world
inside the war inside the egg
inside the sea, on a bench at the edge
of the lake, demi-baguette drooping from his coat
and a mallet in his pocket for chistling
his mind's next eye, he dreams a tiny countryside,
a topaz duckling, a miniature golden track,

a bitsy goat in a red scarf, riding in a train car
just like a lady, the single jade tulip,
a silvered pussywillow, snowdrops of amethyst
poking out of the earth. All of it, gone,
merde. I am dying, he thought,
tearing off a bit of baguette and feeding it
to the sleepy mallards at his feet. O shabby heart.
Years ago, he kneeled before the Tzarina,

his hand trembling as she opened the first orb.
Inside, a yolk of gold.
Inside the yolk, a sleigh.
Inside the sleigh, an agate crown,
nestled the way he had just in that moment
nestled himself to her happiness; a cameo
wearing a cameo inside a cameo.
Every spring, another—the bejeweled dancer

set in mid-leap, tutu of rose-quartz blooming from the pink shank
of her thigh as she glinted at herself in a mirror the size of a pearl,
the carousel-egg, horses spinning around pea-sized sepia portraits
of the royal family, turning and turning,
closing away from his hands forever.
Then came the steel boots, the bolts, the shattered marble—

his workshop a shambles, his eggs hollow tombs,
his heart blown clean with steam as the last train pulled him west.
Now he is whispering Verdi to the four-o-clocks again

their mechanical petals tilted toward his voice
the way he once tilted upward
as she sweetened his cheek with a kiss
she'd fastened to a leaf and floated down to his face.
He gilded leaves in the night and pinned them to everything;
brooches of hazel on his trousers, pockets lined with linden,
he'd press them to his eyes like gelt, remembering.
Here, moths boil against lamplight
and his heart pumps thin and watery beneath his misbuttoned shirt
as he miters an elegy to the companion of dark tubers
beneath the audience of sky. *Violetta! Violetta!*
It wasn't the quail that he missed most,

fed to him by the palace servants, or the partridges and doves
licked clean of their feathers and stuffed with dates and sugared plums,
the silvery sturgeon plated with its span of fins,
or the warm hearth licking the grouse filled with currants, the silk sheets,
not the quiver of Turkish rose-jellies on tiny spoons that jellied in his throat
when she entered the room—

no, it was the dust that would rise up in the shop after sautering,
the light that poured through the windows out into the snowdrifts,
the way birdcherries flowered the city in the warm wind
and the petals would stick in her hair, that moment
in spring when he began to grow the next tiny world,
its doorposts and its ice slides,
its glockenspiels and its lilacs, the madness

that rose inside him as he watched her tug at the velvet,
unlocking his new little planet—
he would have cracked his own sternum
if his heart had been the rubied surprise inside.
At the edge of this alien lake, the hens of his hands lay only pebbles.
O shale heart. Here, he was the last man ever, tzar of himself,
king of rubble, the tail of a kite escaping

from a cheap plaster shell, fluttering through the chestry oaks,
pulled by some invisible wind, through the soot and haze
and coppery light, toward a ceiling of cumulostrata,
sadness coiling up the lattice and into the memory
of what was once invention and desire
and now was stopped like a waterclock,
starving for rain.

DONOVAN ORTEGA

In a Large Coastal City

IF YOU FIND YOURSELF DRUNK, high, and kicked out of a halfway house in a large coastal city that you know to be called Boca Raton—take heart. Your stay will be wonderful.

Do not worry if this is your first time being a vagrant. There are many seasoned drifters who started out as displaced drug addicts. It will simply require small adjustments in lifestyle. It may be time that you embraced homelessness.

You'll be happy to know that despite Boca Raton's wealth, there are plenty of McDonald's. With the last of your cash, treat yourself. Peruse the dollar menu. Choose from an assortment of these tasty items: the McDoubles, the McChickens, even a sweet fruit parfait, or a side salad. Order cookies. All meals ought to end with cookies.

Celebrate your new freedom.

Eat the McDouble on a bench along Federal Highway and look at luxury cars. Try and finish your food in one sitting. Once it is in your belly, you can think of something else.

Cigarettes—bum them at bus stops. Always offer to pay, but know that no one wants your change.

If you are alone, do not sleep in parks. Even in Boca Raton, parks can be dangerous. They are filled with vagrants probably hungrier than you.

Which is why you need to make friends with other street people. Just because you are homeless, does not mean you have to live without friends.

Drink malt liquor with them behind the CVS on Glades Road. After you are finished with your beverage and feeling levitated, you can beg for change.

James Rutherford Park is a lovely place to spend the day. You can recline with raccoons beneath the mangroves, look out upon the Intracoastal Waterway and watch the yachts float by.

But do not stay in one place for too long. The Boca Raton Police Department does not want you to get comfortable, so practice becoming invisible. Do not panhandle at intersections. You will get money, but you will also get a reputation. Never forget that, as you traipse through the streets disheveled, you are probably ruining someone's lunch.

Learn a pointless skill to peddle. Make roses from the husks of palm trees. Create bouquets and sell them to the lovely young couples coming out of the bars in Royal Palm Plaza. Approach the boys. They'll want to impress their dates. Sell the bouquets for five dollars, but accept anything.

Throw a party for yourself. Go to a McDonald's restaurant and order this: two Mc-Doubles, no pickles, ketchup, or mustard. Add Mac Sauce and shredded lettuce. Each McDouble is one dollar. Shredded lettuce and Mac Sauce is an additional thirty cents. The total comes to $2.60. Discard one half of one the buns and slap the sandwiches together to create a Big Mac that costs about four dollars on the regular menu. Eat it on a bench or in the grass. Watch the cars, watch the yachts. Enjoy the Big Mac.

But remember this: it is important you not appear ridiculous. Try and take a bath in the ocean at least once every two weeks. If you need to use a plastic bag to store your things, only use one. And don't ever push a shopping cart down the street; it is a surefire indication that you have lost your mind.

Nevertheless, when the city has taken its toll, get bed rest. Go to Boca Raton Regional Hospital and claim that you want to kill yourself. They'll admit you to the psych ward and you'll get off the streets for a few days.

I think you will find your experience of Boca Raton very different from the one you may have heard about.

Boca Raton is a place that people discuss as if it were an amusement park, a country in Epcot. They'll recount a tired narrative about rich women who dress up their dogs like children. They'll drone on and on about fake tits, plastic hips, liposuction, and Botox. They'll tell you about the rich geriatrics and their beautiful young wives, or how the sixteen-year-olds drive BMW's to school. They'll tell you that Boca Raton is a plastic city, a place that the rich come to retire so they can die in the tropics.

But understand, as you push your shopping cart and carry plastic bags across an intersection of brick pavers, that there are so many different kinds of misery in the world.

About once or twice a year, someone throws themselves in front of the train that runs along Dixie Highway. The roads are closed for hours so the police can investigate and remove the body.

And in the winter of 2010 it was so cold in Boca Raton—in the thirties and forties well into March—that the iguana population was decimated.

Frozen iguanas dropped from the trees.

The iguanas are making a comeback now, though. You'll see them, sometimes, sun tanning on the banks of canals. I'm beginning to notice them, more and more.

There are, of course, many halfway houses in this city—hidden in plain view as apartment complexes and single family homes—and if you want to avoid vagrancy, you can be sure that someone will give you another chance, provided you have the cash or kind, northern parents that are flush with currency and just want to see their sweet drug-addicted child get better.

But if you do not want to be homeless and do not want to get better, do not waste your time in halfway houses or twelve step meetings.

Get on Craigslist and find a room to rent. There are so many rooms to rent and so many people in Boca Raton that will listen to your sad story.

If you have a job, try your best to keep it.

After you lose it, call your kind northern parents that are flush with currency and just want to see their sweet drug-addicted child get better. Ask them to wire money.

Get as fucked up as possible.

Don't waste your time with the synthetic drugs at gas stations—the Kratom and the Spice won't get you to the edge of oblivion and that is what you should try and do.

If you like alcohol, drink long and drink for the effect.

If you cannot find heroin, switch to pills.

Doctor shop. Clinics line the streets and they are filled with physicians that want to help you with your pain.

Clean your needles. Hepatitis C is contracted through old, rotted blood.

Find a friend, any friend. No matter what, it's always good to have a friend.

When you lose that friend, find another.

Tell your Craigslist family you are trying to get a job. Call your kind, northern parents that are flush with currency and just want to see their sweet, drug-addicted child get better. Ask them to wire money.

Get as fucked up as possible.

Rob your drug dealer.

Get as fucked up as possible.

Invade a home and steal some minor heirlooms.

If you are not prepared to do that, maybe this life is not for you.

Prick yourself with dirty needles.

Have unprotected sex you cannot remember.

And when you are arrested, evicted, beaten, raped, robbed; when your Craigslist family has had enough; when your kind, northern parents that are flush with currency cut you off; when everything you own is in a shopping cart; when you, for the first time, understand what it is to be thirsty—take heart.

Every day can be a holiday in this large coastal city.

From atop a parking garage in Mizner Park, I watched the Fourth of July explode over the campus of Florida Atlantic University. From the roof of the garage, I could see every fireworks demonstration between Deerfield and Delray Beach. Boca Raton's finale made the night glow white—for fifteen seconds it looked like the end of the world.

And I have kissed a Jewish girl I hardly knew underneath the Christmas tree in Mizner Park. She thought it romantic, how we made out on a bench in the golden, red and green twinkle. And despite my skepticism, even I felt blessed. "Joy to the World" played from speakers disguised as Christmas presents and, from within the compound of Mizner Park, I could forget that you might be drunk in a gutter, still outside and without home.

·

BUT IF A PECULIAR THING happens and you find yourself struck sober in this large coastal city—take heart. Your stay will be wonderful.

Get on your knees and say a prayer. Even if you do not believe, say a prayer.

Get a job, any job. It doesn't matter what you do. It only matters that you work.

Call your kind, northern parents that are flush with currency and just want to see their sweet drug-addicted child get better. Tell them you are alive and end the conversation. When they offer you money, tell them no.

Find a twelve-step meeting. It does not matter which, it only matters that you go. You can recognize the meeting places by the giant plumes of smoke rising from the thresholds of churches and clubhouses, fifty cigarettes burning simultaneously, magical wands rising and falling in angelic choreography.

Be faithful to a divinity, any divinity. Understand that you have taken your place inside the celestial blueprint. Angels and spirits guide your feet.

Walk or ride or crawl—a combination of all three. It doesn't matter which. It only matters that you move.

Know that you are exactly where you need to be. If you were supposed to be somewhere else, you would not be in this large coastal city.

But don't be too proud—all you did was stop killing yourself.

Buy a bicycle. Do not steal it.

Ride your bicycle around the city: west on Glades Road to Military Trail, south on Military and then rock east upon Camino Real. Ride by your old Craig's List family home and wave, keep moving east—pump the pedals all the way to A1A and hit that beach road at twenty-five miles an hour. Take it all the way to Delray with the wind at your face.

Go to a twelve-step meeting.

Try very hard not to judge the people that you meet there. Try very hard to keep an open mind about the people sitting in those windowless rooms. Even that lady next to you, the one wearing the red hat and a shirt that's seven sizes too small—she too, is a personification of God.

Your life depends on this belief.

Even after your bike is stolen and you lose faith in those windowless rooms and the cigarettes and the damned book and everything that I have told you to hold sacred— move about this large coastal city and seek something that you can understand.

Purchase another bicycle.

Mount the contraption that is rusty and blue with a chain that clink-clanks and a seat that shakes.

Name it Rusty Blue.

Resent that you have to ride a bicycle, but ride it anyway.

Stop at all intersections. Obey all traffic laws. The street signs will ooze by. Every crack in the sidewalk will feel like a small catastrophe, but do not consider them this.

Get faster. Pedal harder. Soon, you will not notice the cracks. Careen over them. Find purpose in the rhythms.

Do not stop at intersections. Dive through traffic and wave at the cars that stop in your powerful wake. Abandon the sidewalk. Crash onto the road and needle a path between the white line and the grass. There isn't a bike lane and you shouldn't care. Fuck the bike lane.

You're a rusty-blue blur against the black asphalt that hugs the edge of the world.

And this is you at your best: on Rusty Blue pumping those piston legs, not caring about anything but speed and that strange hope in something you cannot see. Hold onto this conviction.

Scoff at those who say Boca Raton is only pavers and landscaping. Scoff at the nay-sayers who insult your city.

Go west on Spanish River Boulevard. Behold Pondhawk, a 79-acre wetland preserve that lies just north of the Spanish River Library. Behold the Mediterranean Revivalist architecture of the library, the brainchild of Addison Mizner, Boca Raton's architect and the namesake of our lovely park.

No, the library is not some ancient Spanish village that sits upon a cliff with a transcendent ocean view. But it is all we have and it is time you learned to recognize the sublime. Your life depends on the skill with which you observe.

Buy a coffee and a cookie—they make them fresh in the library café. Go out on the covered patio and sit at the iron tables beside the Corinthian pillars. Drink the coffee. Smoke a cigarette. Eat the cookie. Everything is better with a cookie.

Look out on the perfect roundness of Blue Lake. Observe the anhinga and mottled duck and great egret. Forget that the lake is a manmade product of IBM's 1970 headquarters. It is a lake and it is blue. It is as authentic as it will ever be. And it attracts birds that don't know the difference; to them, water is water and land is land.

All kinds of things are drawn to Boca Raton—the old and wealthy, the empty and thirsty, the beautiful and feathery.

Ride your bicycle, rusty and blue, along the path that encircles Blue Lake.

Behold the light, the way it strikes the red-shingled roof of the library. Behold the anhinga that soars and then nose-dives into the lake filled with fish that swarm beneath its blue waters. Behold all these things at once as you push your bicycle down the path and into Pondhawk.

I can remember when the preserve was not finished, when it was just a construction site, a chaotic bramble. A girl I once loved was among those who helped to create it. She removed invasive species that sprang up between the pond apple trees and slash pines. She pulled Old World climbing ferns from the ground. With a machete, she cut down Brazilian peppertrees at the stump. She did these things and told me about them and, for the sake of love and her pretty face, I was interested.

She taught me to bird watch, to recognize the anhinga and the mottled duck and the great egret. She taught me other birds too, so many I cannot hope to remember them all.

My eyes followed her finger when it pointed.

Look, she said, and I looked.

Behold the colored birds on their stilt legs. Try hard to appreciate their beauty—it is impossible to know where girls go when they disappear north, to the Middle West.

And sometimes, when I'm driving a car that is dented and rusty and blue, I remember her pretty face and the finger that pointed in the glimmer of those first sober days. Do you know what bird that is? she asked.

Yes, it is the most beautiful bird, I said. It is the purple gallinule.

Find a purple gallinule: yellow tipped and red beaked and brilliant yellow feet; green and blue feathers that glow.

You can find them foraging for food in the shallows, at the roots of fireflags.

That's the most beautiful bird, she said.

It is the most beautiful bird, I agreed.

And just yesterday, I was at Pondhawk sitting in the gazebo and the sun was setting. Fish jumped in the pond below and within the water grasses I could hear the wading birds call out. With their peculiar squeals and guttural squawks, they sang and I was filled with birdly mysticism.

I peered into the shallows, and I looked for a purple gallinule.

The birds cried so loudly last night, I could barely hear the cars on Interstate Ninety-Five.

Translation Folio

CORSINO FORTES

Translator's Introduction

Sean O'Brien

CORSINO FORTES IS A LEADING Cape Verdean poet of the "liberation" generation, a left-wing modernist born under colonial Portuguese rule. Written in a combination of Portuguese and Creole, his poetry deals with oppression and colonialism while sustaining a visionary sense of a re-made African-Atlantic of the future world where the wrongs of the past will be undone. Rich in marine and archipelagic imagery, both epic and local in their sense of scale, the poems pursue a densely allusive "logic of the imagination" while moving between vivid observation and impassioned declamation.

The challenge for poets making English versions of Fortes' work is to accommodate the elevated, exclamatory character of the poems without sounding empty and inflated, as surrealism (a clear reference point) often does in English. Against this, Fortes marshals an extraordinarily subtle, sustained and powerful rhythmic life, able to speak to the auditory imagination of the non-Lusophone. The impression is of magnificently controlled lyric improvisation.

The literal versions were supplied by the translator Daniel Hahn, who was extremely helpful in clarifying ambiguities and obscurities where possible. Despite this there are inevitably moments in the present renderings of the poems where the passage of sense from one phrase to the next relies on instinctive association or juxtaposition rather than a settled interpretation. There are symbolic "sets" in Fortes which seem to have no equivalents in English, and in these cases the authenticity of the rhythmic impulse has been privileged.

CORSINO FORTES : Five Poems

Embarking

There is fever now
        fever in the gum
The coat of sweat
         cooling the teeth
The corncob
        in the scorched mouth
The bay sweating
          sun and sunflower

I left the plumb-line
              on the steps of the city
I left the hammer and the anvil
              in the council chambers
I left the pestle and the mortar
              Under your face: Monte Cara
And on the wild surge of the waters
I packed my stuff
         And left
The heart behind and sailed to larboard

But before long before
I mortgaged
           my litre of blood
And left

I planted my thumb
        beside your tree
          o idol of my little earth

In that lesson
Of earth & blood
                              Transfused
The heart wild with the sea's surge
        From the heart to larboard

Postcards from the High Seas

I

Crioula, you will tell the guitar
Of the night, and the dawn's small guitar
That you are a dark-skinned bride
                with Lela in Rotterdam

You'll never sell around the town
                From door to door
The thirst for sweet water that slaps
                In a tin can

II

In the morning
It snowed on the temples of Europe
The lamp of my hand is a caravel
                Among the fjords of Norway

Since yesterday
It's been raining on the prow
                Steel rain that numbs
Our abandoned bones
                gnomon of silence without memory

Since yesterday
The ship is the landscape of a blind soul
And your name upon the ocean
                the sun in a fruit-tree's mouth

III

I used to sell Kamoca
                On the streets of New York

I've played ourin among the girders
        Of skyscrapers under construction

In a building in Belfast
Remain the skulls and bones
          Of my contemporaries
The blood remains
          Alive in the telephones' nostrils

IV

The ears of the islander heard
The sun-drenched voice in the Olympian throat
Of a pestle in Finland

I saw patricians
          clad in togas
Speaking Creole
In vast auditoria

       Beyond the Pyrenees
        there are blacks and blacks
Immigrants to Germany
       in the soup-making countries
the blacks of Europe

V

Crioula, on Sunday evenings
         with the sun on the bushes
You will say to the good-natured faces
        Of old cricket-players
That the names
         Of Djone
           Bana
           Morais
           Goy
           Djosa

                                        Frank
                                        Morgoda
                                        Paliba and Salibana
Present themselves
            as
                        white stamps on documents
            as
                        passport and laissez-passer

            At the doors of the embassies

VI

Our mouths testify
            that the earth and the story
Emigrate with us under our tongues
To witness
            the dry knees and elbows
                        of the colony of Cabiri

VII

Along the chemins-de-fer
                        I give blows and receive them
From the locals
over land disputes
                        And cultural norms

In a night of lunacy
            In the colony of Sacassenje
We divided the land
            Between fruit-trees and seeds
            Between blood and scars

Having foreseen this I stayed at the border
Gripping the lock of my door

VIII

Now as I walk
I watch the birth: the spring that watches
The shade of the shoulder-blades over the world
Striking the drum
       with the blood of Africa
       with the bones of Europe

       And

Every evening my thumb returns
       And says to the mouth of the river
       From Addis Ababa I came and drank
       In the cataracts of Ruacana

Emigrant

Every evening, sunset crooks
        its thumb across the island
And from the sunset to the thumb
        there grows
        a path of dead stone
And this peninsula
        Still drinks
All the blood of your wandering body
From a tenant farmer's cup

But when your voice
        becomes a chord on the shore's guitar
And the earth of the face and the face of the earth
        Extend the palm of the hand
From the seaward edge of the island
        A palm made of bread
You will merge your final hunger
        with your first

From above there will come
The faces and prows of not-voyage
        So that herbal and mercury
Extract the crosses from your body

The screaming of mothers carries you
        now
To the seventh corner
        where the island is shipwrecked
        where the island celebrates
Your daughter pain
The pain of a woman in childbirth
So that all parting is power in death
        All return a child's learning to spell

No longer do we wait for the cycle
    Pulp from good fruit, fruit from good pulp

The earth
    admits
        your green phallus

And there before your feet
    Should be
        A tree on a hill
And your hand
    Should sing
        A new moon in my belly

Go and plant
    in dead Amilcar's mouth
This fistful of watercress
And spread from goal to goal
    A fresh phonetics
And with the commas of the street
    and syllables from door to door
You will sweep away before the night
The roads that go
    as far as the night-schools
For all departure means a growing alphabet
    for all return is a nation's language

They await you
    the dogs and the piglets
    at Chota's house
    grown thin from the warmth of the welcome

They await you
    the cups And semantics of taverns

They await you
    the beasts
    choking on applause and sugarcane

They await you
    faces that explode
    on the blood of ants
    new pastorals to cultivate

But
       when your body
             of blood and lignite, on heat
Raises
             over the harvest
Your pain
And your orgasm
                  Who didn't know
                  Who doesn't know
                           Emigrant
That all of parting is power in death
And all return is a child learning to spell

Gate of the Sun

I

From the straw hills
     whose gates are the sun
Children descend
    naked and thin
      like guitars
ribs showing under the strings
All of them
   the first-born
     of the one belly
And daughters
   of the same volcano And of the same guitar
   Of the same rock and the same cry

II

The island revolves in the face of its child
There's a stick jammed in the wheel of the wind

III

The child does not
Always breathe
    its lung was
      torn from the map
And thus
   like the islands themselves
At sunset
They are fed
    on phonemes
Each child
Is a diphthong of milk
    with blood in its vowels

Act of Culture

How the sound swells in the fruit: the drum
                              Is on the tree
And opposed to erosion: the politics of seduction

                    And

"If the destiny of man is ceaseless labor"

                    And

The word love has no mouth to its river

Culture! is entirely
Old chaos given dynamic expression

Translated from the Portuguese
by Daniel Hahn & Sean O'Brien

D. A. POWELL

I Also Do Impressions

I am a restless soul born of a restless man
who wandered in and out of time.

He appeared to die across the phone,
his unbearable breathing.

So little to do at the end of things.
This isn't about that man
but what became of his son.
This kid could listen
to Journey or the Temptations.
Although he preferred Temptations.

For he was born under the sign of "Yield."
This is what I can do well, he thought,
here is my pass.
                  He had to pass,
although he grew up in a white world.
Not quite white in the head, though.

And so he learned "Any Way You Want It"
and other white hits.

He learned them from
a blue-eyed meth addict he was attracted to.

He learned them from the johns
who sang so tragic:
Teenaged wasteland
It's a teen-aged wasteland

and naught comes from a wasteland
but waste.

Waste, you see, is wasted
on the young.

To Carthage then I came
where round about me and on every side
there sizzled such a skillet of
Temptations
doing "Papa Was a Rolling Stone"
and any place I laid my hat
I was bound to be bare-headed.

He struggled with that.
A city is an orgy that
just hasn't started yet.
They're sizing you up.

Lord I wouldn't take nothing
for my Journey records now, but

sometimes you just gotta go
it's a ball of confusion.

-

AARON SMITH

Lessons

In my father's retirement
he's learning to play
the banjo. Two hours each day:
"runs" and "vamping"
in the back of the house. He goes to camps
where they teach him to play by ear:
Something has to click.
When I took piano as a kid,
he never wanted to listen, attended
recitals because mom forced him. Relieved
when I finally quit: *Such a sissy instrument.*
Now there's something innocent
in the way he talks, a gentleness
I've never found in men:
From your last visit to this one,
am I getting better? I'm happy
to lie, to say yes. I'm not a father.
I don't have to be cruel.

MARK HALLIDAY

Doctor Scheef

Doctor Scheef you probably tried hard
in 1971 at your clinic in Bonn
I assume you tried hard to save my mother
with your regime of enzyme injections
and 30 million units of Vitamin A

but you did not save my mother—
at best you gave her a little hope for a while
though I suspect she was too skeptical even for that
though she tried to believe for my father's sake;

Doctor Scheef you needed to be a historic genius
but you were not!
                              And so my mother went on hurting
month after month with cancer in her vertebrae and her spine
and she died after three more years of hurting
since you were not a historic genius Doctor Scheef
—and you must be dead by now too
and forgiving you would make sense no doubt
but I'm not ready, maybe I am not yet tired enough
so I prefer to name you here sternly

rather than settle for the letting go in forgiveness
as I am still in the non-genius condition of wanting
targets for complaint therefore I say that in 1971
you should have been a hell of a lot smarter Doctor Scheef.

NICK LANTZ

Reenactment of the Battle
for the Planet of the Apes

The old battlefield is a national park.
Tourists line the outer fences, taking pictures
to show to their relatives back home.
The reenactors of the Great Ape Regiment
wait on the hill, polishing their period-accurate
laser rifles, while in the old stream bed below,
Bravo Company pulls on their human masks,
tugging at the rubber cheeks until the eyeholes
line up just right. It's an honor to play
the doomed *Homo sapiens* troops,
who, in a few minutes, will go charging
up the hill, only to be cut down.

"We respect the humans' bravery,"
says the tour guide standing beside
the Statue of the Unknown Human Soldier,
"but evolution doesn't second-guess itself."

One boy's father buys him a plastic
human skull at the museum gift shop.
All the way home, the boy holds the skull,
runs a finger along the smooth crown
where the saggital crest should be,
works the jaw up and down, as if
teaching the forgotten how to speak.

SALLY KEITH

from River House

21.

Poem I wrote for my mother to say to me:

Sweet child I made of fire, sweet child, little fire
Bedeck the world with angels and ladders

Little mirror, I give you my last ounce of breath
I give you my breath to be emptied of life

Here, little fire, here, here
Little fire lift my hand to feel a body emptied of life
Lift my hand, little mirror

Little fire, sweet child
Put flowers on top of the table
Little fire, light candles in churches and cathedrals

Fire catches, sweet child
Bedeck the world with angels and ladders
Climb, little fire, climb higher and higher

I made you like this, little mirror, listen
As the wind shifts, listen to the smallest drops of water

from River House

25.

When my mother came home for the first time
She stood at the front door and wept.

Otherwise, she didn't complain, at least not to us.

The five-month story of the time she was sick
Would be impossible to recount. My problem is
I don't know what to do with it.

Do you know how many millions of organisms
Exist in a single spoonful of ocean water?

It's inimitable, utterly impossible to recreate.

I remember my father telling us he had begun
To like the hospital, the little city of it. We practiced

Imagining ourselves as biological mass.
My father's skeleton even seemed to have shrunk.

I remember one day over a cafeteria lunch
His sobbing, head collapsed, the doctor having asked
My mother her opinion about current events.

from River House

61.

Really there is no one we want to take to the river with us.
There is nothing to do there but nap, eat, and drive,
White Stone, Kilmarnock, Irvington, a triangle.

Along the roads there water seeps in like mirrors
Reflecting back rings of wild.
At a certain place you can stop to hear the peepers.

"A strong song tows us," writes Basil Bunting.
It feels like something once stacked is seeping.

At the edge of the stage a masked actor is standing.
She practices experiencing.
Breathes. Tries to let out the tension in her shoulders.

Told to imagine the freighter departing, she imagines
The freighter an inch adding thickness to the line called horizon.
The space between the mask and her face is a metaphor for living.

She waves good-bye.
She is practicing waving.

MARK BRAZAITIS

The Ease of the Explorer

IN SANTIAGO, THE SKY WAS the gray of an uncertain hour. For the second straight afternoon, Jay found a seat at a table in the corner of what his guidebook called the "Poets' Café" because Pablo Neruda had stopped here once to piss and wrote a haiku on the bathroom wall. If the old men in the café were poets, they had left their notebooks and pens behind. There were three of them, a pair playing chess beneath a stained-glass window in front and the third at a table next to Jay's. The third was fair-skinned and thin-faced, and he had wrinkles like watermarks in the sand. He wore an olive green, long-sleeved shirt and a tan, herringbone jacket.

The waitress, a pale, tall woman with a high hairline, brought Jay's coffee and two empanadas de pino, filled with beef, onions, and raisins. The day before, he'd talked to her about Neruda and his three houses in Chile and all his famous friends. He thanked her now and smiled and she smiled back.

With his round face, like a moon with freckles, and reddish-orange hair, Jay looked, in the words of a woman he'd dated in his last year of college, "like everyone's twelve-year-old cousin," which made her want to pinch his cheeks, she said, but not to sleep with him. To the waitress, he said, "You look like a dancer."

She eyed him suspiciously, but perhaps responding to the openness of his face, she smiled again and said, "I am studying ballet."

He asked her where, and she told him. He asked her if she had any upcoming performances, and she said, "In two days, in the Teatro Santa Inocencia." She waited as if he might ask another question. But he thought of Consuela, his girlfriend, and looked down at his journal and she retreated.

Every so often, the man next to Jay glanced at him.

Two months earlier, Jay had finished his Peace Corps service in Guatemala. Instead of heading back to the States, he'd cashed in his plane ticket, taken a third of his $7500 readjustment allowance in traveler's checks, and traveled south—by bus, boat, train, and whatever vehicle would pick him up on the side of the road—stopping wherever he wanted, sometimes for a few hours, sometimes for a few days. His next stop would be over the border in Mendoza, Argentina. After he saw Tierra del Fuego, his trip would be complete.

He had told his parents he would use his trip to think about what to do next with his life, and they had supported his plan with encouraging words and permission to use their credit card, should he need to. In truth, he was traveling because several of his Peace Corps friends who had finished their service before he did had done so and had raved about their experiences and because he thought it would be fun to tell people he had been to the end of the earth and because he had nothing better to do.

In the Peace Corps, he had been a 4-H leader, teaching schoolchildren how to grow vegetable gardens and build compost piles and make re-hydration solution out of water, sugar, and limes. He couldn't exactly turn these skills into a paying job back home in Ohio. He fantasized about writing travel stories and selling them to *The New York Times*. He'd never written a published word in his life.

The old man at the table next to him caught his eye. "You are writing the great American novel?" he asked, his accent pronounced but intelligible.

"I wish," Jay said.

"So you are from the CIA?"

From the man's tone, Jay didn't know whether he was joking. In Guatemala, Jay had been accused, and not always in jest, of being a spy. During long nights in his block house in the western highlands, he'd read books he'd come across in the Peace Corps library on the history of Latin America and its troubled relationship with the United States. Given the CIA's role in overthrowing its president, Salvador Allende, in 1973, he knew Chile had as much reason as Guatemala to be suspicious of gringos.

"You are taking notes," the man said, nodding toward Jay's diary. Covered in blue-and-white Guatemalan tipica fabric, it had been a present from Consuela before he left Guatemala. The two of them used to spend every Friday and Saturday night in the park in Zunil, kissing. She was Evangelical and hoped he would marry her. He liked her. Maybe he loved her. But he didn't have a job and he wasn't sure what he wanted to do or where he wanted to live.

"It's only a journal," Jay said.

"So you are a journalist?" the man said, perhaps misunderstanding, perhaps making a joke.

Jay nodded vaguely, thinking this might end the conversation.

"Perhaps you'd like to hear my story," the man said. The old man motioned him over. Obligingly, Jay stood, picked up his journal, and moved to the man's table. Jay introduced himself, and the old man did the same. His name was Maximo. As they sat across from each other, Maximo asked Jay if he'd seen a certain movie about the disappearance of an American during the overthrow of Allende. Jay said he had, a couple of weeks before he'd left Guatemala. He'd been staying in Antigua, the country's old capital, and it had been raining one evening when he'd ducked into an open doorway. The owner of the house, a man from Nebraska, was showing *Missing* to a tour group and invited Jay in to watch it on his large-screen TV.

"I was with the American the night he died," Maximo said.

"In the National Stadium?" Jay asked.

"What you don't understand from the movie is the smell of the place. The sweat. The shit."

Maximo spoke slowly, sometimes pausing for a word. "For most of the night, I was sitting next to him in a room without windows. It was quiet except for the sound of dripping water." He sighed. "He told me he was sure he would be released. 'I am an American,' he said—like this made him invincible. He said he was worried about me. Would I be all right?"

Maximo frowned, his wrinkles deep. "I didn't think so. But I said, 'No problem. They have the wrong man.'"

"Did they?" Jay asked. "Did they mistake you for someone else?"

"They were cruel but they were not stupid. In a sense, they did have the wrong man—every one of us. Because what were we doing? Only everything we could to make the lives of workers and campesinos better."

"It's like what I did in the Peace Corps, in Guatemala," Jay said. "I taught children how to make their lives better." He understood that his life as a norteamericano in Guatemala, someone whom the Peace Corps would have pulled from the country at the first sign of a coup, and Maximo's life as a supporter of a besieged government were far from identical. But he was hoping to impress the old man, to show him they had common ground.

They talked a little about Jay's work in Guatemala before Maximo said, "I was sure I was going to die. To be tortured and killed. But it was my American friend who was called first by two soldiers at the door."

"Jesus," Jay said. "And you? What happened to you?"

Slowly, Maximo pulled his hands from under the table. He spread his left hand in front of Jay. The top of his index finger had been sliced off. The partial finger was darker and redder than the rest. Jay nodded to show he understood.

Maximo shrugged. "To lose only the tip of a finger? I was lucky. I could have lost everything." He withdrew his hands, concealing them again under the table. "It must be nice to live in a country where war is always somewhere else."

"I never thought about it," Jay said. His Guatemalan friends had been reluctant to discuss with him their experiences in the country's civil war, probably because of Consuela, whose father had been a captain in the army. At age fifty-one, he was retired now, living in the family's two-story house behind a black, wrought-iron fence. Three German shepherds patrolled his yard.

"It's all right," Maximo said. "Why should you?" He excused himself, stood, and shuffled toward the men's bathroom. Presently, the waitress returned. "Has my grandfather been telling you fables?" she asked.

"Fables?"

"Stories about the overthrow of Allende."

"Yes. Terrible." Jay shook his head.

"It was his son—my uncle—who was tortured in the National Stadium during the coup. Afterwards, he was never the same. This was thirty years ago, before I was born. My uncle died three weeks ago. He lived with my grandfather all this time."

"I don't understand. I mean, what about his—your grandfather's—finger?"

"An accident at work." She glanced toward the men's room. "Did I hear you say you are a journalist? It wouldn't be right to report what he said as fact." She paused. "My family thinks he has gone crazy with grief, pretending to be his son so his son will never die."

"I think there's a scientific term for it." He wasn't sure this was true. But he was trying to be helpful.

"Here he comes," the waitress whispered. In his two days here, he had neglected to ask her name. She disappeared into the kitchen.

Maximo returned to his seat. "So you lived in Guatemala. They've had worse troubles than we Chileans. How long was their war? Thirty, forty years? You must have heard stories."

He couldn't say he had. He thought of inventing a story. Consuela's father sprung to mind as a villain, ordering the execution of campesinos. The vision troubled him because it might be true. In the end, he shrugged and said, "I'm only a naïve gringo." This is what Consuela's brother had called him. He had darker skin than she or her parents, and Jay saw him around town sometimes standing out of the rain under tienda rooftops, smoking cigarettes with other men whose eyes simmered with disdain. "My father and brother," Consuela told him, "fight like rabid dogs."

Jay's father was a vice president at Sherman Savings and Trust, which somehow had avoided being devoured by larger banks. His mother worked as a librarian at Ohio Eastern University. His parents owned one car between them and drove to work together every morning. His sister was a senior at Ohio State and was the president of her sorority. When he was in Guatemala, he'd written to his parents and his sister every week, filling pages with minute by minute, or at least hour by hour, descriptions of his days. He described the food he ate in Zunil's comedores; the compost piles he built with his 4-H groups; the games of ping-pong he played with the two brothers who lived in the house next to his. He saw now how tedious his letters must have been.

Again, he thought of inventing a conversation he might, under different circumstances, have had about Guatemala's civil war. But again nothing came to mind. He pictured his weekend nights on park benches with Consuela, her hand resting on his shoulder as if they were dancing a waltz.

Maximo said, "The heart hurts to know the suffering of good people."

Jay nodded, as if he understood in the way Maximo did.

"But tell me something else, something happy. Did you fall in love?" His smile wrinkled his face in a new way. "With Rigoberta Menchú, perhaps?"

Jay had heard a hundred jokes about the Nobel Prize winner. It seemed to be a Guatemalan sport to jab their most famous countrywoman. "She's prettier than people think," he said.

"With all her Nobel money, she is gorgeous!" Maximo said and laughed. "But en serio, did you fall in love?"

One Saturday, two months before he left the country, Jay and Conseula went to Quetzaltenango to see a matinee at the Teatro Municipal. It was a student performance that ridiculed Guatemalan politicians and generals and the United States government. Consuela hated it and was surprised Jay didn't show the same disgust. He explained: Even if he was a Peace Corps volunteer, his government had nothing to do with him. Whether his country was benevolent or evil, he told Consuela, "my hands are clean."

They were sitting in the park, in front of the Hotel Bonifáz, its yellow exterior glowing in the late afternoon light. "I've always wanted to stay here," she said, nodding toward the hotel. "To have a room with a balcony overlooking the park."

"Let's do it," he said. "Let's rent a room."

She looked at him, half appalled, it seemed, half curious.

"You can tell your parents you're staying with Olivia tonight." Olivia taught in a Spanish language school in town. Jay was surprised by how quickly he composed a plan, as if he'd plotted it days before. "I'll go rent the room now. Wait here." He stood and moved toward the hotel. He turned around, giving her a chance to protest. Her expression was unreadable. He proceeded to the hotel, where his parents' MasterCard bought a night in a room with a balcony.

A minute after they'd stepped into the room, they were lying on a double bed under a painting of a volcano, kissing like it was their last day on earth. The pleasures they'd been unable to partake of on park benches were available to them now. When he had her shirt off and her pants down to her knees, her only words were, "This means you will marry me."

His agreement had been the act itself, repeated later the same night and before breakfast the next morning. Neither of them had once mentioned protection, but what, he'd thought after they'd returned to Zunil, were the chances?

"Yes, I fell in love," Jay said to Maximo.

"Many times, I hope."

He had promised Consuela he would return to Guatemala immediately after he reached Tierra del Fuego. He'd made the promise because it was easier than not making it.

"Once," Jay said.

Maximo smiled. "Once can sometimes be enough."

In Buenos Aires, Jay stayed in the Lime House Youth Hostel. He shared his room, which contained three bunk beds, with five other travelers. There was a pool table in the middle of it. On his first night, he was awakened at midnight by a pair of his roommates, brothers from Norway or Sweden, playing eight-ball. When he mumbled a complaint, one of the brothers said in English, "You're in Argentina, bro. Bedtime is six in the morning."

On the second day, Natalia, the woman at the front desk, who wore a girlish pink ribbon in her black, curly hair, asked him if he'd like to see *Eva: El Gran Musical Argentina*. The hostel had been given free tickets, she explained. Natalia's eyes were large and luminous, like a child's witnessing something remarkable. "Will you be going?" he asked.

"I wish," she said. "But I need to be with my children."

"You have children?" he asked, failing to conceal his surprise.

"Three," she said.

"You're young to have children," he said.

"I'll be twenty-seven in two weeks." She handed him a ticket. "Eva Perón was thirty-three when she died."

In the Teatro Lola Membrives, Jay sat in the back of the upper mezzanine next to a woman in glasses and her husband or boyfriend, who was punching numbers on his cell phone frantically, as if desperate to place a last bet or sell a last stock before the house lights expired. The woman told Jay she was here because her office had free tickets. "I've heard it's propaganda," she said in a soft voice. "But the singing is supposed to be beautiful."

If the Andrew Lloyd Webber *Evita* portrayed Argentina's most famous woman as more sinner than saint, *Eva* left out the sinning altogether. There was no selling her body to climb to the top. There was only ideological fervor, her life as pure as fire. The light dimmed only when she was diagnosed with cancer, and even with cancer she behaved like a benevolent goddess.

"If only it had been so," his seatmate whispered to him as Nacha Guevara finished her last stirring song.

Jay wandered into the night, feeling restless. He thought he could do something he'd never done: drink his way to oblivion, sleep with a prostitute. But when a man with beard stubble and a cigar handed him a pamphlet for a strip show featuring a pair of women with moon-sized breasts, he crumpled it up and threw it in the nearest trashcan.

The following morning, a Saturday, he decided to call Consuela. He used to own a cell phone, but it had fallen out of his pocket somewhere in Panama City. He found a Telefónica in a YPF gas station on Avenida Córdoba. The glass booth he was assigned smelled like empanadas and sweat. He was nervous as he punched in her number. Her father answered. He wanted to know all about his trip. He said, "Be careful of the tango dancers—they might dance away with your heart." He asked, "When are you coming back?"

Before long, Consuela was on the phone. She said hello, then, "Un momento, querido." He heard her ask her father for privacy. He heard her father jokingly complain. Then he heard a door shut. "Jay?" She still didn't know how to pronounce the 'J' correctly. It sounded as if she was saying "Hey."

He asked her how she was doing. They spoke in Spanish. Her English was so-so. There was a short silence. He heard her cup the phone's mouthpiece. Her voice was a whisper: "Jay, I'm pregnant." A pause. "I'm scared." Another pause. "Will you come back now? If my father finds out . . . We need to be married. Soon."

"Pronto," Jay repeated mechanically, as in a language class.

"Married as soon as you come back. Like we talked about . . . like you said."

"Pronto," he said again.

"I miss you. I love you."

Jay's thoughts were a car on ice, sliding fast and out of control. *I don't believe it. This can't be happening. I don't believe it.* He remembered their room in the Hotel Bonifáz. When night fell, she'd stood naked at the window and he'd wrapped his arms around her from behind, dipping his head into her hair.

"I love you," he said, repeating the words he'd spoken as he smelled her hair, as if he and Consuela were still in the hotel room, as if all that lay before them was a sweet, inconsequential night. He heard his voice echo somewhere in the miles, the kilometers, between them. It sounded as if he were speaking from the bottom of a deep well.

"You'll come back today or tomorrow, Jay, won't you? I can't sleep. I've been so nervous."

"I'm going to Tierra del Fuego. I bought the plane ticket yesterday. It's the end of my trip."

"But afterwards, you're coming back here, aren't you, querido? Please?"

Before he could say anything, there was a snapping sound, like a band being cut, and he heard a dial tone. "Hello? Hello?" All he heard now was the echo of his voice, sounding confused and lost. He hung up.

When he stepped out of the booth, the man who ran the Telefonica office asked him if he wanted to try the call again.

"Later. Thank you," Jay said and paid and returned to the street.

TIERRA DEL FUEGO WASN'T A land of fire but of cold wind and smoke-gray skies. It shared a frigid, watery border with the end of the world. He couldn't imagine how the early settlers to the place had survived. They would have had to acquire new skills quickly, and they either learned from their mistakes or died from them.

Standing on the south coast of La Isla de Los Estados, the penguins they had been promised nowhere in sight, his clothes wet where his undersized rented rain gear had failed, Jay wondered how he'd managed to come so far without being touched by cruelty, malice, or misfortune. No one he knew had died. His grandparents were still alive. They were happy, healthy. His parents had had all of four arguments in their lives. His sister—

What would they say if he told them Consuela was pregnant? They knew her only as a name written in his neat cursive in his boring letters. In his correspondence, he hadn't made much of her.

On his flight to Ushuala and on his overnight boat ride here, he had avoided thinking about it all. He had imagined he was finishing his journey the way he long conceived he would, with the carefree ease of an explorer and not the burden of a settler. But no matter what he did now, whether he returned to Consuela or to the States, he would feel the weight of his decision, of his responsibility or his irresponsibility. What's more, he had the feeling he would discover things he'd overlooked in his life, things painful and troubling he'd seen in his periphery but hadn't bothered to examine. They would be waiting to inhabit him. He remembered Maximo, haunted by his son's suffering. He remembered the children he'd taught in Guatemala and what their families had certainly suffered during the war. He remembered Consuela's brother, his cool independence, his bitterness toward his father.

I'll have a child soon.

He turned from the thought. But as the wind from the South Pole chilled his face, he knew he had run out of room to roam, to run. Soon, the horn would sound, and he would board the dinghy, then the ship, and head north again. Even so, he lingered, gazing south at the watery horizon. He imagined his journey continuing, propelling him until he fell off the end of the earth and floated away, free and untouched, swimming in space toward stars.

CRAIG MORGAN TEICHER

Poem About Everything

Oh, it'll be alright—it always will
and was; it just takes a certain
or uncertain (because the clock's behind
a curtain) span of time for the cup
to fill that catches and collects
the tears and tap water and
glintings of sunlight in dewdrops

on the window sill. And once
it's full again—which may take
years or decades or epochs
of man—we can rest assured
that whatever set all this in motion—
be it deity or the selfless will
of biology that initiated wars and

trees and weekends and paramecia—
is proceeding according to its
plan. We may not be aware
that this change has taken place
—no one anyone knows or can fathom
will still be alive—but we will share,
distantly, in a kind of celebration

over the knowledge that existence
continues to thrive. It has on Mars
where basins, once oceans, are found,
and silence, or the soft knock
of colliding particles of windswept
dust has replaced what we think of
as sound. Existence continues, whether

or not we are to blame
for whatever interruptions
its progress needs, and hope will keep
crawling from the ooze, festering
like weeds. This news is good:
everything is unfolding slowly,
excrutiatingly, just as it should.

ERIKA MEITNER

Insane Flying Machines

What's in the box? Tonight's present contains
10 wings, 10 tails, 10 rudders, 2 fuselages
for assembly. We turn off NPR in the middle
of the train derailment story—four dead,
maybe faulty brakes to blame—and congregate
to bless the candles, which flare orange

and run wax rivers onto the counter, until
they eventually extinguish themselves
in delicate curls of smoke. Because the Gemara
says place the menorah next to a window
facing the street, we also twist the orange bulbs
of my grandmother's plastic electric on the sill,

left over from a time when plugs had two prongs,
which makes me nervous, since the local news
is all house fires and break-ins until Christmas.
The Gemara says in times of danger, placing
the menorah on a table indoors will suffice.
At Hanukkah we celebrate the Maccabees,

their victory over the forces of King Antiochus,
or the miracle of the temple oil lasting and lasting.
Danger includes all types of danger—the local
student who set himself on fire concocting
Butane Hash Oil, those people on the train.
What's in the box? Weary commuters

sleeping with ear buds, leaning their heads
against the windows on a Sunday while
a conductor works his way down the aisle

with his hole punch. What's in the box?
A metal xylophone and a yellow mallet.
Together they play music. Earlier today,

my son sits on my lap in a booth lined
in carpet while an audiologist—a woman
with very straight hair the color of butterscotch—
talks to him, makes boxes hung in each corner
light up when she says his name from one speaker
or the other. Levi, she says, again and again

into her microphone. Before his name was Levi,
it was King. What's in the box? Antiochus.
Us. We watch her lips through plexiglass,
but it's not clear if he can actually hear her words
from the right or left, though he looks sharply
when one speaker, for a moment, pops static.

In the next room the doctor tells me my son has fluid
behind both eardrums and says his son is adopted too,
from Utah, and he thought about naming his son
Utah, but his wife intervened. Interventions are,
by their very nature, dangerous: that train—
the news says some passengers were flung

from the windows. The news says the less wounded
helped the more seriously injured. One car nearly
went into the river, but it didn't. I do not want
my son to be put under, to get tubes in his ears.
He is scooting everywhere, takes four steps
at a clip, isn't yet a year, presses his small hand hard

to the lump that's grown above my breast and below
my voice box. My mother beat breast cancer
and now sees a meditation teacher at Memorial
Sloane Kettering to calm herself as part of some
kind of holistic wellness program, but her teacher,
Robert, does not often calm her when she's

on the phone yelling, if you visit that bitch, don't bother
coming home, and then hangs up on me. She is talking
about my aunt, her dead-to-her sister, and when
I recount her anger to friends they counter
with tales of aunts and grandmothers who hold
similar vendettas—this fierceness that grows,

rather than dulls, with age. What's in the box?
An entire series of Captain Underpants books,
a nerf turbo football, a keyboard made of electronic
flowers. My sister and I discuss my mother at length
behind closed doors, and every time, it ends in
what's in the box? The Holocaust, our grandmother's

time in the camps. The Gemara says danger includes
all types of danger, like gentiles stealing lights, or
throwing stones. War, scarcity, oppression, darkness.
Hanukkah and Thanksgiving won't intersect again
for 76,000 years, and there are my sons—
the older assembling cardboard airplanes,

the younger pressing rainbow flowers which sound
notes of electronic joy. What's in the box? Anger
that does not dissipate with time. Chaos. Bubble wrap.
Hot Wheels. A plastic racing track. We are fine.
We are not fine. This holiday of miracles or war
or light, depending on the year, the spin.

NICOLE SEALEY

Candelabra with Heads

[AFTER THE SCULPTURE BY THOMAS HIRSCHHORN]

Had I not brought with me my mind
as it has been made, this thing,
this brood of mannequins, cocooned
and mounted on a wooden scaffold,
might be eight infants swaddled and sleeping.
Might be eight fleshy fingers on one hand.
Might be a family tree with eight pictured
frames. Such treaties occur in the brain.

Can you see them hanging? Their shadow
is a crowd stripping the tree of souvenirs.
Skin shrinks and splits. The bodies weep
fat the color of yolk. Can you smell them
burning? Their perfume climbing
as wisteria would a trellis.

as wisteria would a trellis.
burning? Their perfume climbing
fat the color of yolk. Can you smell them
Skin shrinks and splits. The bodies weep
is a crowd stripping the trees of souvenirs.
Can you see them hanging? Their shadow

frames. Such treaties occur in the brain.
Might be a family tree with eight pictured.
Might be eight fleshy fingers on one hand.
might be eight infants swaddled and sleeping.
and mounted on a wooden scaffold
this brood of mannequins, cocooned
as it has been made, this thing,
Had I not brought with me my mind

Who can see this and not see lynchings?

LAREN McCLUNG

Gowanus, Brooklyn

Go back to Vermeer's maps
   for a clue of how they travelled
to tidal creeks & swamplands
   where the Canarses chief fished
the new moon's falling tide
   for bay angler & blue crab.
He sold ground for copper pots,
   cardamom, nutmeg, Chintz,
& knives with boxwood hilts
   carved into a lion's head.
Granite blocks steadied the fluyts
   as ballasts that later paved roads
beside the canal where horses
   pulled barges along the harbor.
The Fourth Street Basin oysters
   flourished in the brackish water
where African fishermen harvested
   for the Dutch, pickled, & shipped
to Barbados supper for the Great Gang
   who cut cane for rum or sugar
to sweeten English tea & cakes.

Where I stand, men built their masters
   stone houses & tide-water gristmills.
Owning begins with felled trees & language—
   Breukelen, Rood Hoek, Konijneneiland.
In a new swap for kettles & hatchets
   the Natives hunted beaver & marten
no longer found here for fur coats & hats.
   But time moves like the East River
Washington's troops once crossed
   to flee Red Coats. Now the city speaks

in plaster fortified with strands of hair
    from a local barber shop swept clean—
men & women without headdress
    caught in the walls of an apartment
where shadows move in the half-light.

Here before a cabinet of wonders,
    a Belgium block, a diaper pin,
the old world made visible,
    all at once I see a boy on a Thursday
playing seesaw, balanced on a plank
    until he vanishes into the canal.
Apparitions of wild horses search
    for corn husks, potato peels, or scraps
but find no salvation, no milkweed,
    gamma grass, bittersweet nightshade—
& before the skull of the minke whale calf
    once trapped in the broken waters
one knows what will not come back here.

Arvonia

The neon wings of bluebirds break by a sign
posted "Solitude" at the edge of a dirt road

& cyclops moths stare out from the pines.
There is no way to turn back as I reckon

the light of Mercury in the west horizon.
Oh, late June, magnolias summon the dead

who once pinned a bloom in her hair
as if ferried back through a natural gate.

This ancestor I have known in the faint light
where her face appears as smoke drifting.

Virginia, what sickness sleeps in the air
where torn sheets hang from a tree branch?

I've seen the white bull grazing on this path,
& what they say is true, there's only one way past.

Yes, I've brought back the horns as proof.

REBECCA HAZELTON

The Underwater City

You were happy, and thus, suspect. Inquiries were made.
Your weight and height were measured at different times,
under varying conditions. In a park on a beach towel
laid out in the sun reading you were exactly the same length
as on a bus scaling a hill listening to music on the way
to work. It seemed impossible. Further examinations
yielded more data, less certainty. Your hair showed
no signs of recent drug use, the salt and pepper ratio
consistent with previous readings. Your tongue was soft
like a mouse stripped of skin. When you undressed
for inspection, one breast was slightly larger than
the other but then, it had always been so. The bellybutton
was properly tied off. The moles did not correspond
to any star patterns in the western hemisphere,
and were disregarded. But there were disturbing readings.
When you took a shower the water was punishingly hot.
You picked at the cuticle of your right thumb, deforming
the nail bed. A habit, you said, but why had it developed?
Your stools were firm and regular, which was irregular.
Your eyes were, one researcher noted, *furtive*, a word
he'd never used before in a report. He was quarantined.
But you were happy. You smiled on the 4th of July
for no patriotic reason. Footage from the grocery store
showed you joking with the butcher. Shows your teeth
white against your skin, your skin unblemished, unpicked.
You walked with purpose, even if that purpose
could not be quantified. When you drove to the ocean
and swam out to the sandbar, you were far enough
from shore to only register on the instruments as a dot
then a line then a streamer, waving. After that,
nothing. There was the usual seaweed, phosphorescence.
Observers found washed up on the beach two jellyfish,

assorted clam shells, a sun-bleached condom, one fish head. Science cannot tell us if drowning is best under current human subject guidelines. There is theory, and there is practice. You were happy. Were you happy?

SARAH ROSE NORDGREN

Animal Space

The bush sings brightly by
the lane, dispersing
its hundred invisible cheeps to the air.
Behind the leaves you can see
the hundred birds hung
through a vast, enveloping network
like the scientist who,
after treatment, gained depth
perception for the first time
and while walking home
from teaching at the university
was amazed by the opening
of the trees which now held
"pockets of space" between the leaves,
and in winter by how she was now
a part of the voluminous
snowfall instead of just watching it
on a movie screen like she'd done
her whole life. The proportions
of animal space grew around her head
so now she could locate her deep
ancestors, as well as those relations
who never were—every one
of earth's species surrounded by a cluster
of impossible monsters. She saw
the real animals dotted
here and there throughout the air,
but fell in love with those hypothetical ones
who perched at their shoulders
like angels or entourages.

Pillar of Fire by Night (*Columna ignis nocturna*)

After Johannes Jacob Scheuchzner's Physica Sacra

There is a black side and a white side of sleep
knitted up the center in a column

keeping watch over you, traveller,
as you slumber darkly in your hut.

The white side gathers all your breaths
and funnels them into the great lung

outside your body, alternately calling forth
and forcing back a stream of air.

The black side is the pilot light
burning in the earth three feet below

your cot. The low down tug of heat.
How long will you lie there with

the miles pulled tight in your sheet?
A little sleep, a little slumber, a little folding

of the hands to rest. I see you from above
and at a distance west, your hut among

hundreds, while the pillar pluming over camp
rifles your notebook and ledger pages.

ALAN MICHAEL PARKER

The Last Page

I have stopped reading the last page of novels—
now the horse drags the rider down the lane

and through the sugarcane field
to the impossibly brown sea

and that's where they stop, just short.
Now the sun turns to look.

I have stopped believing what's next:
I have laid down my knitting of time.

I have left the pillowcase off
of the perfect afternoon.

As for the final square of chocolate,
stay there uneaten, my shiny, silver joy.

I have stopped smoking every cigarette.
I have stopped cutting the cut grass.

Oh, little bird, abide with me
before the stars go out,

before the handle turns,
before the floorboards creak awake,

before anyone rises to a bell.
Pertaining to the spirit, I can only suggest

try a cool washcloth for the heat.
I have driven off without my change,

stopped one block shy
of the last block on earth.

Mom, go back to your hospital room, your lilac
nightgown still on your small shoulders.

Bios

A member of the Squaw Valley Community of Writers, **HEATHER ALTFELD** teaches at California State University, Chico. Recent poems are out or forthcoming in *Narrative Magazine, The Literary Review, Pleiades, ZYZZYVA, Poetry Northwest,* and others. She just completed her first manuscript of poems.

MICHAEL BAZZETT's poems have appeared in *Ploughshares, Massachusetts Review, Pleiades, Oxford Poetry, Hayden's Ferry Review* and *Best New Poets*. He is the winner of the Lindquist & Vennum Prize for his first full-length collection, *You Must Remember This* (Milkweed Editions, 2014).

MARK BRAZAITIS is the author of five books of fiction, most recently *The Incurables: Stories* (U of Notre Dame Press, 2012), winner of the 2013 Devil's Kitchen Reading Award in Prose, and *Julia & Rodrigo* (Gival Press, 2013). His collection *Truth Poker* won the 2014 Autumn House Press Fiction Competition and will be published in 2015. He is Professor of English at West Virginia University.

JOEL BROUWER teaches in the creative writing program at the University of Alabama. His fourth full-length collection, *Off Message*, is forthcoming from Four Way Books in 2016.

CATHERINE BREESE DAVIS (1924–2002) published poems in such places as *Poetry, The Southern Review, The New Yorker, The Paris Review,* and *New Poets of England & America* between 1950 and 1998. A collection of her poems, accompanied by essays about her life and work, is being edited by Martha Collins, Kevin Prufer, and Martin Rock, and will be published in the Unsung Masters series in June 2015.

KENDRA DeCOLO is the author of *Thieves in the Afterlife* (Saturnalia Books, 2014), which was selected by Yusef Komunyakaa for the 2013 Saturnalia Poetry Prize. She is the recipient of awards from the Tennessee Arts Commission and the Breadloaf Writers Conference and residencies from the Millay Colony and the Virginia Center for Creative Arts. She is a visiting professor at Sarah Lawrence and lives in Nashville, Tennessee.

The recipient of fellowships from the Wisconsin Institute for Creative Writing and the Provincetown Fine Arts Work center, **LAURA EVE ENGEL** has published poems in *Black Warrior Review, Boston Review, Crazyhorse, The Southern Review, Tin House,* and elsewhere. She is the Residential Program Director of the UVA Young Writers Workshop and lives in Brooklyn.

MATTHEW FERRENCE lives and writes at the confluence of Appalachia and the Rust Belt. He is the author of *All-American Redneck: Variations on an Icon, from James Fenimore Cooper to the Dixie Chicks* (U of Tennessee Press, 2014), and his nonfiction has appeared in *Colorado Review*, *Gettysburg Review*, *Gulf Coast*, and elsewhere. He teaches creative writing and literature at Allegeny College.

ROBERT LONG FOREMAN has published fiction and nonfiction in *Agni*, *Indiana Review*, *Massachusetts Review*, *Michigan Quarterly Review*, *Third Coast*, and *The Pushcart Prize Anthology*. He teaches at Rhode Island College.

CORSINO FORTES, born in 1933, is a Cape Verdean writer who has authored three collections of poems. For more on Fortes, see page 135.

JOHN GALLAHER's fourth and fifth poetry collections are *Your Father on the Train of Ghosts* (BOA Editions, 2011; w/ G. C. Waldrep) and *In a Landscape* (BOA Editions, 2014). He teaches at Northwest Missouri State University and co-edits *The Laurel Review*.

JENNIFER GROTZ's third book of poems, *The Window Left Open,* is forthcoming from Graywolf Press in 2016. She teaches at the University of Rochester and serves as the director of the Bread Loaf Translators' Conference.

DANIEL HAHN has translated several books by the Angolan novelist José Eduardo Agualusa, most recently *Rainy Season* (Arcadia Books, 2009) and *The Book of Chameleons* (Simon & Schuster, 2008), which won the Independent Foreign Fiction Prize. He has also authored several works of nonfiction and serves as Chair of the Society of Authors in London.

MARK HALLIDAY teaches at Ohio University. His sixth book of poems, *Thresherphobe*, was published in 2013 by the University of Chicago Press.

REBECCA HAZELTON is the author of *Fair Copy* (Ohio State UP, 2012) and *Vow* (Cleveland State UP, 2013). She was the 2010-11 Jay C. and Ruth Halls Poetry Fellow at the University of Wisconsin and winner of the "Discovery"/*Boston Review* 2012 Poetry Contest. Her poems have appeared in *Agni*, *The Southern Review*, *Best New Poets*, *Best American Poetry*, and *The Pushcart Prize Anthology*.

HENRY ISRAELI is the author of three full-length poetry collections, including, most recently, *god's breath hovering across the waters* (Four Way Books, 2016; forthcoming) and *Praying to the Black Cat* (Web Del Sol, 2010). He has also translated three books by the Albanian poet Luljeta Lleshanaku, most recently *Haywire: New & Selected Poems* (Bloodaxe, 2011) and *Child of Nature* (New Directions, 2010). He is the founder and publisher of Saturnalia Books.

The recipient of fellowships from the Stanford Humanities Center and the Guggenheim Foundation, **TROY JOLLIMORE** has published two poetry collections: *At Lake Scugog* (Princeton UP, 2011) and *Tom Thomson in Purgatory* (MARGIE/Intuit House, 2006), which won the 2006 National Book Critics Circle Award. His third collection, *Syllabus of Errors* (Princeton UP, 2015) is forthcoming.

SALLY KEITH's third and fourth collections are *The Fact of the Matter* (2012) and *River House* (2015; forthcoming), both from Milkweed Editions. Keith teaches in the creative writing program at George Mason University.

DAVID KEPLINGER's fourth poetry collection is *The Most Natural Thing* (New Issues Poetry, 2013). The recipient of fellowships from the National Endowment for the Arts, the DC Council on the Arts and Humanities, and the Soros Foundation, he teaches at American University.

MELISSA KWASNY is the author of five books of poetry, most recently *Pictograph* (Milkweed Editions, 2015), *The Nine Senses* (2011), and *Reading Novalis in Montana* (2009). She is also the author of *Earth Recitals: Essays on Image and Vision* (Lynx House Press, 2013) and editor of *Toward the Open Field: Poets on the Art of Poetry 1800-1950* (Wesleyan, 2004).

The recipient of the Great Lakes Colleges Association New Writers Award and the Larry Levis Reading Prize, **NICK LANTZ** is the author of three poetry collections, most recently *How to Dance as the Roof Caves In* (Graywolf Press, 2014). He teaches at Sam Houston State University.

HAILEY LEITHAUSER is the author of *Swoop* (Graywolf 2013), which won the Poetry Foundation's Emily Dickinson First Book Award. Her work has recently appeared or is forthcoming in *32 Poems, The Gettysburg Review, Poetry, The Yale Review*, and *Best American Poetry 2014*.

ALEX LEMON's fourth poetry collection is *The Wish Book* (Milkweed Editions, 2014). The recipient of fellowships from the NEA and the Minnesota Arts Board, Lemon is also the author of two nonfiction books: *Happy* (Scribner, 2009) and *Migrants in Feverland* (Milkweed; forthcoming). He teaches at Texas Christian University.

TRUDY LEWIS is the author of three books of fiction, including *The Bones of Garbo* (Ohio State UP, 2003) and the forthcoming *The Empire Rolls* (Moon City Press, 2014). She teaches at the University of Missouri.

ADA LIMÓN's third and fourth poetry collections are *Sharks in the Rivers* (Milkweed Editions, 2010) and *Bright Dead Things* (2015; forthcoming). She divides her time between Lexington, Kentucky, and Sonoma, California.

RANDALL MANN is the author of the poetry collections *Straight Razor* (Persea Books, 2013), *Breakfast with Thom Gunn* (U of Chicago Press, 2009), and *Complaint in the Garden* (Zoo Press, 2004). He works in biotech and lives in San Francisco.

ADRIAN MATEJKA's three poetry collections are *The Devil's Garden* (Alice James Books, 2003), *Mixology* (Penguin Books, 2009), and *The Big Smoke* (2013), which won the 2014 Anisfield-Wolf Book Award and was a finalist for the National Book Award and the Pulitzer Prize. Matejka is the recipient of fellowships from the Guggenheim Foundation and the Lannan Foundation and teaches at Indiana University, Bloomington.

LAREN McCLUNG is the author of the poetry collection *Between Here and Monkey Mountain* (Sheep Meadow Press, 2012). She teaches at NYU.

KATE McINTYRE's work has appeared most recently in *Denver Quarterly*, *The Collagist*, and *Cimarron Review*. She teaches at Allegheny College.

ERIKA MEITNER's fourth book of poems is *Copia* (BOA Editions, 2014). She teaches in the graduate writing program at Virginia Tech and is currently a Fulbright Distinguished Scholar at Queen's University Belfast.

MIGUEL MURPHY is the author of *A Book Called Rats: Poems* (Lynx House Press, 2005), which won the Blue Lynx Prize.

SARAH ROSE NORDGREN is the author of *Best Bones* (U of Pittsburgh Press, 2014). Her poems have appeared in *Agni*, *The Harvard Review*, *The Iowa Review*, *The Literary Review*, *Ploughshares*, *Best New Poets*, and elsewhere. She teaches at Miami University of Ohio, Middletown.

MICHELLE OAKES has recent poems in *The Laurel Review*, *RHINO*, *Ruminate*, and others. She lives in Houston, Texas, where she recently received an MFA from the University of Houston, and where she works for the Writers in the Schools program.

NATHAN OATES is the author of *The Empty House* (U of Washington Press, 2012), and his stories have appeared in *Alaska Quarterly Review*, *The Antioch Review*, *The Missouri Review*, *Witness*, and elsewhere. He teaches at Seton Hall University and lives in Brooklyn.

SEAN O'BRIEN is the author of six poetry collections and has won numerous national prizes in the UK, including the T. S. Eliot Prize and the Forward Prize for *The Drowned Book* (Picador, 2007). He teaches at Newcastle University.

DONOVAN ORTEGA is an MFA candidate in fiction at Florida Atlantic University. After graduation, he plans to ride a bicycle from Key West to Seattle. This is his first publication.

ALAN MICHAEL PARKER's seventh poetry collection is *Long Division* (Tupelo Press, 2012). His third novel is *The Committee on Town Happiness* (Dzanc Books, 2014). He is Douglas C. Houchens Professor of English at Davidson College, and also teaches in the University of Tampa's low-residency MFA program.

CATHERINE PIERCE is the author of two books of poems, *The Girls of Peculiar* (Saturnalia, 2012) and *Famous Last Words* (2008). Her work has appeared in *The Best American Poetry*, *Slate*, *Boston Review*, *Ploughshares*, *Field*, and elsewhere. She is an associate professor at Mississippi State University, where she co-directs the creative writing program.

D. A. POWELL's most recent collections are *Useless Landscape, or A Guide for Boys* (2012), which received the National Book Critics Circle Award in poetry, and *Repast* (2014), both from Graywolf Press. He lives in San Francisco.

Poems by **NICOLE SEALEY** have appeared in *Callaloo*, *Harvard Review*, *Ploughshares*, *Best New Poets 2011*, and elsewhere. The recipient of the 2014 Stanley Kunitz Prize for Younger Poets from *American Poetry Review*, she is the Programs Director at the Cave Canem Foundation.

AARON SMITH is the author of *Appetite* (U of Pittsburgh Press, 2012) and *Blue on Blue Ground* (2005). His work has appeared in numerous publications, including *Court Green*, *Ploughshares*, and *The Best American Poetry 2013*. He teaches at Lesley University in Cambridge, Massachusetts.

CRAIG MORGAN TEICHER is the author, most recently, of *To Keep Love Blurry* (BOA Editions, 2012) and *Ambivalence and Other Conundrums* (Omnidawn, 2014). He is currently editing the selected writings of Delmore Schwartz for New Directions and at work on a collection of essays due out from Graywolf in 2017.

JAN WAGNER, born in 1971 in Hamburg, Germany, is a German poet and author of four collections. For more on Wagner, see page 47.

ALLISON BENIS WHITE's poetry collections are *Small Porcelain Head* (Four Way Books, 2013) and *Self-Portrait with Crayon* (Cleveland State UP, 2009). Her poems have appeared in *American Poetry Review*, *Indiana Review*, *The Iowa Review*, *Ploughshares*, and elsewhere. She teaches at the University of California, Riverside.

STEFANIE WORTMAN's first book of poems, *In the Permanent Collection*, was selected for the Vassar Miller Prize and published by the University of North Texas Press in 2014. Her poems and essays have appeared in *Yale Review*, *Michigan Quarterly Review*, *Boston Review*, and other publications. She lives in Rhode Island.

Required Reading

(Issue 20)

(We asked that the issue's contributors recommend up to three recent titles. This is their list.)

Michelle Alexander, *The New Jim Crow: Mass Incarceration in the Age of Colorblindness* (Joel Brouwer)

Abdul Ali, *Trouble Sleeping* (David Keplinger)

Bernardo Atxaga, *The Adventures of Shola*, trans. Margaret Jull Costa (Daniel Hahn)

Nicholson Baker, *Traveling Sprinkler* (Robert Long Foreman)

Hadara Bar-Nadav, *Lullaby (with Exit Sign)* (Allison Benis White)

Paul M. Barrett, *Glock: The Rise of America's Gun* (Randall Mann)

Max Barry, *Lexicon* (Donovan Ortega)

Joshua Beckman, *The Inside of an Apple* (Ada Limón)

Selected Poems and Some Prose by Gottfried Benn, trans. Michael Hofmann (Miguel Murphy)

Eula Biss, *On Immunity* (Robert Long Foreman, Sarah Rose Nordgren, Stefanie Wortman)

Malachi Black, *Storm Toward Morning* (Sarah Rose Nordgren, Michelle Oakes)

John Branch, *Boy on Ice: The Life and Death of Derek Boogaard* (Alex Lemon)

Geoffrey Brock, *Voices Bright Flags* (Randall Mann)

Lucie Brock-Broido, *Stay Illusion* (Ada Limón)

Cynthia Carr, *Fire in the Belly: The Life & Times of David Wojnarowicz* (Aaron Smith)

Eleanor Catton, *The Luminaries* (Katharine McIntyre)

Cathy Linh Che, *Split* (Laren McClung)

Carolyn Chute, *Treat Us Like Dogs and We Will Become Wolves* (Trudy Lewis)

Jeffery Conway, *Showgirls: The Movie in Sestinas* (Aaron Smith)

Averill Curdy, *Song & Error* (Hailey Leithauser)

David J. Daniels, *Clean* (Jennifer Grotz)

Geffrey Davis, *Revising the Storm* (Erika Meitner)

Erica Dawson, *The Small Blades Hurt* (Alan Michael Parker)

Kendra DeColo, *Thieves in the Afterlife* (Adrian Matejka)

Natalie Diaz, *When My Brother Was an Aztec* (Catherine Pierce)

Kerry James Evans, *Bangalore* (D. A. Powell)

Tarfia Faizullah, *Seam* (Adrian Matejka)

Harrison Candelaria Fletcher, *Descanso for My Father* (Matthew Ferrence)

Carrie Fountain, *Instant Winner* (Erika Meitner)

Elisa Gabbert, *The Self Unstable* (Rebecca Hazelton)

Celeste Gainey, *The Gaffer* (Aaron Smith)

John Gallaher, *In a Landscape* (Troy Jollimore)

Douglas Goetsch, *Nameless Boy* (Mark Halliday)

Rigoberto González, *Unpeopled Eden* (Ada Limón)

David Graeber, *Debt: The First 5,000 Years* (Joel Brouwer)

David Harsent, *Fire Songs* (Sean O'Brien)

Endi Bogue Hartigan, *Pool [5 choruses]* (Laura Eve Engel)

Yona Harvey, *Hemming the Water* (Adrian Matejka)

Rebecca Hazelton, *Vow* (Stefanie Wortman)

Cynthia Marie Hoffman, *Paper Doll Fetus* (Nick Lantz)

Cynthia Hogue, *Revenance* (Alan Michael Parker)

Chloe Honum, *The Tulip-Flame* (Laura Eve Engel)

Rebecca Gayle Howell, *Render/An Apocalypse* (D. A. Powell)

Mark Irwin, *Large White House Speaking* (David Keplinger)

Tove Jansson, *Sculptor's Daughter* (Heather Altfeld)

TJ Jarrett, *Zion* (Kendra DeColo)

Miranda July, *The First Bad Man* (Alex Lemon)

Han Kang, *The Vegetarian*, trans. Deborah Smith (Daniel Hahn)

Sally Keith, *River House* (Jennifer Grotz)

Karl Ove Knausgaard, *My Struggle, Book One: A Death in the Family* (John Gallaher)

Noelle Kocot, *The Bigger World* (Henry Israeli)

Elizabeth Kolbert, *The Sixth Extinction* (Michael Bazzett, Mark Brazaitis)

Keetje Kuipers, *The Keys to the Jail* (Catherine Pierce)

Rachel Kushner, *The Flamethrowers* (Joel Brouwer, Stefanie Wortman)

Ilyse Kusnetz, *Small Hours* (Laren McClung)

Carol Light, *Steam from Heaven* (Hailey Leithauser)

Sandra Lim, *The Wilderness* (Miguel Murphy)

Michael Longley, *The Stairwell* (Troy Jollimore)

Sally Wen Mao, *Mad Honey Symposium* (Kendra DeColo)

David Tomas Martinez, *Hustle* (D. A. Powell)

Jamaal May, *Hum* (Nick Lantz)

Jeffrey McDaniel, *Chapel of Inadvertent Joy* (Kendra DeColo)

Christopher Merkner, *The Rise and Fall of the Scandamerican Domestic* (Nathan Oates)

W. S. Merwin, *The Moon Before Morning* (Melissa Kwasny)

Dunya Mikhail, *The Iraqi Nights* (Laren McClung)

Kyle Minor, *Praying Drunk* (Allison Benis White)

Jenny Molberg, *Marvels of the Invisible* (David Keplinger)

The Star by My Head: Poets from Sweden, trans. Malena Mörling and Jonas Ellerström (Michael Bazzett)

Rusty Morrison, *Beyond the Chainlink* (Melissa Kwasny)

Phong Nguyen, *Pages from the Textbook of Alternate History* (Trudy Lewis)

Renée Nicholson, *Roundabout Directions to Lincoln Center* (Mark Brazaitis)

Yoko Ogawa, *Revenge: Eleven Dark Tales* (Nathan Oates)

Sharon Olds, *Stag's Leap* (Heather Altfeld)

Matthew Olzmann, *Mezzanines* (Nicole Sealey)

Ruth Ozeki, *A Tale for the Time Being* (Trudy Lewis)

V. Penelope Pelizzon, *Whose Flesh Is Flame, Whose Bone Is Time* (Michelle Oakes)

Katie Peterson, *Permission* (Sally Keith)

Carl Phillips, *Silverchest* (Troy Jollimore)

Sara Pritchard, *Help Wanted: Female* (Katharine McIntyre)

George Prochnik, *Impossible Exile: Stefan Zweig at the End of the World* (Miguel Murphy)

Kevin Prufer, *Churches* (Alan Michael Parker)

Sina Queryas, *MxT* (Rebecca Hazelton)

Bin Ramke, *Missing the Moon* (John Gallaher)

Claudia Rankine, *Citizen* (Nick Lantz, Nicole Sealey)

Matt Rasmussen, *Black Aperture* (Henry Israeli)

Roger Reeves, *King Me* (Michelle Oakes, Catherine Pierce)

Robin Robertson, *Sailing the Forest: Selected Poems* (Michael Bazzett)

Marilynne Robinson, *Lila* (Allison Benis White)

Richard Rodriguez, *Darling: A Spiritual Autobiography* (Robert Long Foreman)

Mary Ruefle, *Selected Poems* (Henry Israeli)

Valerie Sayers, *The Powers* (Mark Brazaitis)

Angelika Schrobsdorff, *You Are Not Like Other Mothers* (Heather Altfeld)

Bennett Sims, *A Questionable Shape* (Nathan Oates)

Rebecca Solnit, *Men Explain Things to Me* (Melissa Kwasny)

Peter Streckfus, *Errings* (Sally Keith)

Cole Swensen, *Gravesend* (John Gallaher)

Teffi, *Subtly Worded*, trans. Anne-Marie Jackson, et al. (Daniel Hahn)

Katharine Towers, *The Floating Man* (Sean O'Brien)

Sasha West, *Failure and I Bury the Body* (Erika Meitner)

Caki Wilkinson, *The Wynona Stone Poems* (Laura Eve Engel)

Tony Williams, *The Midlands* (Sean O'Brien)

Hanya Yanagihara, *The People in the Trees* (Katharine McIntyre)

Tiphanie Yanique, *Land of Love and Drowning* (Nicole Sealey)

Kevin Young, *Book of Hours* (Alex Lemon)

Rachel Zucker, *The Pedestrians* (Rebecca Hazelton)

SPRING 2015

the Southern Review

POETRY

Gilbert Allen, Bruce Bond, A. M. Brandt, John Casteen, Carol Ann Davis,
Catherine B. Davis, John Estes, Peter Everwine, Alice Friman, Anna Journey,
Philip Levine, Larry Levis, Joshua Poteat, Thomas Reiter, David St. John,
John Surowiecki, Ryan Teitman, Caitlin Vance, Sally Van Doren

FICTION

Amanda Goldblatt, Peter Gordon, Susan McCallum-Smith, Charles McLeod,
Daniel T. Smith, Saral Waldorf

NONFICTION

Andrew Furman, Georgina Nugent-Folan

VISUAL ART

drawings by Ed Ruscha

INDIVIDUALS: ☐ $40 (1 yr.) ☐ $70 (2 yr.) ☐ $90 (3 yr.) ☐ Sample copy $12
INSTITUTIONS: ☐ $90 (1 yr.) ☐ $120 (2 yr.) ☐ $150 (3 yr.) ☐ Sample copy $24

For orders outside the U.S. add $10.00 per year for postage and remit in U.S. dollars drawn upon a U.S. bank.
338 Johnston Hall, Louisiana State University, Baton Rouge, LA 70803, USA

Look for more information or order online at **www.thesouthernreview.org**

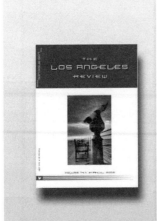

submit now to

GULF COAST ONLINE

RECENT ONLINE CONTRIBUTORS

INTERVIEWS
Megan Mayhew Bergman
Joe Fletcher

FICTION
Penny Anderson
David Hollander
Erin Saldin

NONFICTION
Jim Shepard
Jason Nemec

POETRY
Michael Earl Craig
Joanne Dominique Dwyer
Joe Fletcher
Amaud Jamaul Johnson
Karen Lepri
Geoffrey Nutter
Joni Wallace

Gulf Coast has a new website! We publish exclusive online content and are open to submissions year round. Contributors are paid $50 per poem and $100 per piece of prose. To read recent work, and to submit online, please visit:

GULFCOASTMAG.ORG/ONLINE/EXCLUSIVE/

COPPERNICKEL

subscription rates

For regular folks:

one year (two issues)—$20
two years (four issues)—$35
three years (six issues)—$45
five years (ten issues)—$60

For student folks:

one year (two issues)—$15
two years (four issues)—$23
three years (six issues)—$32
five years (ten issues)—$50

For more information, visit: www.copper-nickel.org.

To go directly to subscriptions,
visit: www.regonline.com/coppernickelsubscriptions.

To order back issues, call 303-556-4026
or email wayne.miller@ucdenver.edu.